Food in a minute®

FAVOURITES

Food in a minute®

FAVOURITES

Celebrating 10 Years

Allyson Gofton

Hodder Moa

National Library of New Zealand Cataloguing-in-Publication Data
Gofton, Allyson.
Food in a minute favourites : celebrating 10 years / Allyson Gofton.
Includes index.
ISBN-13: 978-1-86971-071-2
ISBN-10: 1-86971-071-1
1. Quick and easy cookery I. Food in a minute (Television program) II. Title.
641.555—dc 22

A Hodder Moa Book
Published in 2006 by Hachette Livre NZ Ltd
4 Whetu Place, Mairangi Bay
Auckland, New Zealand

Designed and produced by Hachette Livre NZ Ltd
Photography by Alan Gillard
Photograph of Allyson Gofton by Emma Bass, reproduced with kind permission of *Next* magazine
Printed by Toppan Printing Co., Hong Kong

Front cover: Salami and feta gnocchi, page 50
Back cover: Winter chicken pie, page 115

Contents

Acknowledgements 6
Introduction 7
The making of Food in a Minute 8
Useful information 11

Brunch, lunch & snacks 13

Pizza, pasta, rice, noodles & stir-fries 41

Bakes, braises & pies 65

Roasts & grills 119

Curries 141

Salads & vegetables 155

Desserts & baking 167

Index 205

Acknowledgements

To the whole team at Wattie's — and especially Di Swann for her ongoing support — thank you for the vision to keep producing Food in a Minute. It is still as popular today as when we started 10 years ago. With new products, we keep making it fresh and exciting every year.

I am extremely grateful for the team of girls who have continued to work with me on Food in a Minute. Ann Boardman for her back-up support and stylish and refreshing Food Styling; Sarah-Jane Gillies for her sensational prop hunting, always finding the latest in style; Mary-Lou McGarry, my wonderful PA; and Olwen Edwards for her enthusiastic support. To Alan Gillard, sincere thanks for 10 years of food photography, and how it has changed from involved and detailed to fresh, simple and clean. Thanks also to the many retailers who constantly loan props to us for our film studio and for photography.

Introduction

Welcome to our celebration of 10 years of Food in a Minute. We are very excited that after a decade the programme is still hugely successful and still provides meal inspiration for thousands of kiwis just as it did when it started all those years ago. Over the years of presenting Food in a Minute I have seen our eating patterns change, but most kiwi homes still have one main family meal in some form every day, even though meal times are less structured. People are busier these days, so the dishes that service the family meal have to be more flexible in terms of cost, cooking times, stress and serving sizes — and, of course, still be delicious!

With this in mind, Food in a Minute has kept up by presenting fabulous ideas that suit New Zealanders needs. And we certainly couldn't do this without the help of our sponsors — a big thanks to Wattie's who have been the driving force behind Food in a Minute from the start. Their range of products are such a wonderful assistance in the kitchen, removing much time-consuming preparation from an already busy day and making cooking far more relaxed, fun and tasty. We are also grateful for the ongoing support of co-sponsors Craig's, Eta Foods, Fisher & Paykel Appliances, Kiwi Meats, Mainland Foods, Meadowfresh Foods, New Zealand Pork Board, *Next* magazine, Sealord, SunRice, Tararua and Tegel Foods.

I have been proud and delighted to have presented Food in a Minute to you. The last 10 years has seen much change in food trends and attitudes, but the Food in a Minute team is heartened by the knowledge that New Zealanders still love to cook — and still love Food in a Minute.

Allyson Gofton

The making of Food in a Minute

Director
Graeme Simpson
with Allyson Gofton

Maybe the success of Food in a Minute lies in the old adage 'if it ain't broke, don't fix it'. The programme format has proved to be successful throughout its 10 years but we've taken great care to constantly review and adjust the content to make sure it keeps delivering what you are looking for to inspire your family meal preparation. It's a big job but one that we love.

Food in a Minute is filmed in four batches throughout the year and each filming follows the same process. We begin with the products that the Product Managers have put forward. This can be an eclectic or harmonious mix, meaning that creating recipes is either easy or requires much brain-storming. Mostly our work is seasonally based, though in the case of Christmas, Father's Day and Mother's Day we try very hard to make celebratory programmes, providing inspiration for that special occasion.

Food stylist
Ann Boardman

Once the recipes have been designed by my right-hand food writer and stylist Ann Boardman, (I have chosen to no longer do this so I have more time with my son Jean-Luc), we move to test the recipes. Ann normally does this, though occasionally I get into the act as well. The dish must be worthy of being presented on television and it must also be able to be scripted into a 60-second time frame. That's some asking!

With recipes approved by Wattie's, director Graeme Simpson designs them into scripts. Graeme's our longest serving director on Food in a Minute, so he's become somewhat of a fabulous cook too, in between all his mountain bike riding. At a follow-up script meeting with myself, Ann, Wattie's Food in a Minute manager Di Swann, producer Nick Tapper and account director Andy Robertson we fine-tune the words to fit both the recipes and product's needs. After all, without the products there would be no Food in a Minute.

Sound specialist
Bernie Wright

These scripts then head their way off to the legal beagles to make sure we have not made any claims we should not have. In particular we do this for health claims, as there are strict rules to be followed today. When approval is given there's usually a jump for joy as by now the process has taken about 6 weeks and we can get onto the real work of filming.

Before this happens though, Sarah-Jane Gillies, who has worked on almost every Food in a Minute series, goes shopping. A dream job you might think, but she has to contend with all the Auckland car parking woes and all those shopping bags to carry! Sarah-Jane finds all the plates, props and additional goodies we need to make our Food in a Minute set look modern and have all the items we need to cook with.

Mary-Lou gets to do the supermarket and food shopping so that Ann and I along with Olwen Edwards can get to and prepare the food for the stills photography that is used for the supermarket leaflets, NEXT magazine, the Food in a Minute website and for the books.

Makeup artist
Catherine Stevens

Alan Gillard has been photographing for Food in a Minute for 10 years and has worked with me on all my food photography since 1982! These wonderful pics are constantly inspiring as we keep up with the latest trends on food styling and photography.

The photography is completed the week before we film. Filming starts mid week, Wednesday to Wednesday and we shoot two Food in a Minute segments each day. The set, a 'part-working' kitchen, is supported by our large and spacious prep kitchen, which Ann runs.

Lights are set early by Ado (Adrian Greshoff). Lighting adds mood and also hides the wrinkles that somehow seemed to have appeared over the last 10 years. Ado's attention to details has never waned as he constantly works towards the best light for that particular piece of filming and we all look forward to his rendition of the bird call from National Radio each day.

On sound Bernie Wright has had to record more sizzle, more can or bottle opening shots that you can imagine, yet Bernie has never tired of making sure we make the most of sound — after all, sizzling bacon in the pan is only beaten by its smell.

Behind the camera Ryhs Duncan readies himself for the day. Rhys has been with us from show one and his dedication to eating our ideas has never ceased. We are always grateful to Rhys for this, as he's one of our best critics; and after 10 years he's seen many mince and sausage dishes!

Behind the set is a small make-up room, where Catherine Stevens looks after wardrobe and makeup. Stylist Claire Bridgeman sources the clothes and we begin our week with a try-on (every girls dream) of about 20 outfits to find the nicest 12 that will work well on the set.

That done and dusted Catherine gets on with makeup and hair for the next hour. It's incredibly relaxing having your make-up done which is ideal seeing as the rest of the day is spent under the lights in a tangle of electrical cords required for lighting the set, buckets for washing hands, rubbish bins, products and props. So many times I have wished that we could film the segment showing all the lights, reflectors and sound boom, hovering around a small onion being chopped so that it looks perfect for TV.

Once makeup is finished we get down to filming. Sometimes we are quick and other days we are not, but usually each segment from makeup to completion is about 41/2–5 hours. Ann preps the ingredients that I cook under the lights. Graeme directs each segment to ensure it will cut together in the editing suite the following week, while producer Nick Tapper oversees the whole day's events, dealing with any issues that come along.

With all the programmettes in the can (as the expression goes) Graeme and Nick head back to the editing suite where the material is cut into the perfect Food in a Minute recipe programmettes just for you. The last requirement is sound and I tune in with Neil Newcombe who has sound-edited all 500-odd Food in a Minute tapes over the last 10 years. The voice-overs take about 2 hours. Other than my hello and goodbye, which are recorded at the set, all the other information is dropped in once the recipes have been cut to fit 60 seconds. This includes highlighting any fabulous sounds like sizzles and removing unwanted sounds so it all sounds smooth and effortless. Lastly, the tapes are shipped out to TVNZ ready to go to air.

All of this has taken about 8 weeks and, before you know it, we are back with products getting ready for the next round of ideas.

In between all of this, the recipes and photography has been sent off to designers Oliver Young to be turned into leaflets for supermarket display and dispatched also to *Next* magazine to ensure the recipes appear in the magazine at the same time as they appear on television. The material is also loaded onto the Food in a Minute website. The structure that was set in place 10 years ago to handle the schedule remains pretty much unchanged today, a tribute to Wattie's for understanding your needs when it comes to providing the inspiration to create achievable and cost-efficient, healthy family food ideas — that are also delicious. Thanks Wattie's.

Producer
Mick Tapper

Lighting specialist
Adrian Greshoff

Left: Manager Di Swann
Right: Mary Taylor,
NZ Pork Board

Cameraman
Rhys Duncan

Marmalade steamed pudding, page 202

Useful information

All the recipes in this book have been tested using metric measuring cups and spoons. All spoon and cup measurements are level.

Abbreviations

cm	=	centimetre
tblsp	=	tablespoon
tsp	=	teaspoon
kg	=	kilogram
°C	=	degrees Celsius
ml	=	millilitres

Standard measures

1 cup	=	250 ml		
4 cups	=	1 litre		
1 tablespoon	=	3 teaspoons	=	15 ml
1 dessertspoon	=	2 teaspoons	=	10 ml
1 teaspoon	=	5 ml		
½ teaspoon	=	2.5 ml		
¼ teaspoon	=	1.25 ml		

Approximate metric/imperial conversions

Weight

25 grams	=	1 ounce
50 grams	=	2 ounces
100 grams	=	3½ ounces
125 grams	=	4 ounces
225 grams	=	8 ounces
500 grams	=	1 pound
1 kilogram	=	2¼ pounds

Volume

150 ml	=	¼ pint
300 ml	=	½ pint
600 ml	=	1 pint
1 metric cup	=	250 ml
4 metric cups	=	1 litre
	=	1¾ pints

Measurements

2.5 cm	=	1 inch
10 cm	=	4 inches
15 cm	=	6 inches
20 cm	=	8 inches
30 cm	=	12 inches

Oven temperatures — degrees Celsius to degrees Fahrenheit

Level	*°C*	*°F*	*Gas*
Very cool/slow	110	225	¼
	120	250	½
	140	275	1
Cool/slow	150	300	2
	160	325	3
Moderate	180	350	4
	190	375	5
Hot	200	400	6
	220	425	7
	230	450	8
Very hot	250	475	9
	260	500	10

Chicken in pita with devilled baked beans, page 34

Brunch, lunch & snacks

Apple muesli	14
Breakfast pizzas	16
Father's Day croissants	17
Chuckwagon hash fritters	18
Baked bean hash	20
Corn and bacon fritters on sweet chilli tomato	21
Tropical smoothie	22
Berry nice smoothie	22
Salmon hash cakes	24
Lunchbox roll-ups	25
Asparagus slice	26
Cheat's soufflé	27
Crunchy fish nuggets with dips	28
Pizza pie	29
Mixed bean falafels with minted yoghurt	30
Cheesy corn frittata	32
Winter frittata	33
Chicken in pita with devilled baked beans	34
Chilli Mexicana	36
Mexican tortillas	37
Quick and easy nachos	38
Tex Mex tacos	39

Apple muesli

This recipe appeared in Food in a Minute Book 4 *(2000) many years ahead of going on television. We added extra recipes to Book 4 to create a cookbook with recipes for growing children and this was one of them. Oats are cheap and healthy and contain a yummy type of dietary fibre that helps control levels of cholesterol and sugar in the blood. This muesli can be kept refrigerated for four to five days.*

1 cup rolled oats or flavoured porridge (like Hubbard's fruit porridge)
¾ cup hot water
¼ cup condensed milk
400 gram can Wattie's Diced Apple
1 cup Naturalea Plain Unsweetened Yoghurt
2–3 tblsp honey (use your favourite)
Wattie's canned fruits to accompany

1. In a bowl mix the rolled oats or porridge with the hot water and stand for 3–4 hours or overnight.

2. Mix in the condensed milk, apple and the unsweetened yoghurt.

3. Sweeten with honey to taste, and keep covered in the refrigerator for up to 1 week.

4. Serve topped with yoghurt and fruit.

Serves 8

Breakfast pizzas

Try to use edam cheese on these family breakfast pizzas as it contains 25 percent less fat than cheddar or Colby cheese. Vary the recipe with ham or sliced turkey in place of bacon and add fresh herbs such as parsley, oregano or basil.

4 large pita breads
1 cup Wattie's Tomato Purée or Italian Style Tomatoes
2 cups grated edam cheese
4 rashers streaky bacon, diced
4 eggs

1. Spread the pita breads with equal quantities of either the tomato purée or Italian tomatoes.

2. Scatter the grated cheese and bacon on top.

3. Crack an egg into the centre of each round and season the whole pizza with freshly ground black pepper if wished.

4. Bake at 220°C for 10 minutes until the egg is cooked to your liking and the pizza golden. Cook for 2–3 minutes longer if you like the egg yolks firm.

Makes 4

Father's Day croissants

After this idea aired close to Father's Day in our second year, the sales of baked beans went mad. Most Kiwi dads must have had croissants and baked beans that year to celebrate! The recipe was written with children in mind, hence the preheated oven instruction and cooking the bacon in the microwave.

4 rashers bacon, trimmed of rind
4 croissants
Edam or cheddar cheese
300 gram can Wattie's Baked Beans

1. Heat the oven to 180°C.

2. Place the bacon rashers on a microwave-proof dish. Cover well with absorbent paper and microwave on high power (100%) for 2 minutes. Allow to stand for around 1 minute until cool enough to handle.

3. Carefully cut the croissants on an angle to make a pocket, but do not cut all the way through.

4. Cut thick slices of cheese and place 2 in each croissant. Arrange a cooked bacon rasher on top of the cheese and then spoon in 2–3 tblsp baked beans.

5. Place on an oven tray and cook for 10–15 minutes until hot and golden.

Serves 4

Chuckwagon hash fritters

Perfect for breakfast. The product manager of hash browns (at the time) wanted us to get creative with this freezer favourite and use them in a whole new way. The result was this recipe. It worked very well and is still a fabulously easy idea for a family brunch.

500 gram box Wattie's Hash Browns
1 cup Wattie's Frozen Chuckwagon Corn
4 spring onions, trimmed and finely chopped
½ cup self-raising flour
2 eggs
1 cup milk
¼ cup chopped parsley
1 tblsp mustard (optional)

1. Defrost the hash browns for 1 minute in the microwave, then chop into 1 cm dice.
2. In a bowl toss together the diced hash browns, corn, spring onions and self-raising flour.
3. In a clean bowl or jug beat together the eggs, milk, parsley and mustard, if using. Gently stir the milk into the hash brown mix.
4. Cook large spoonfuls in a hot, greased frying pan for about 4 minutes on each side, turning once only. Serve hot with grilled bacon and golden syrup.

Makes 12

Baked bean hash

From our first book, this easy brunch recipe has proven to be one of our all-time favourites, with many requests for it through our website. It easily combines all your favourite brunch ingredients in one dish. So popular and easy was this idea, that we re-ran the recipe to celebrate 10 years of Food in a Minute.

500 gram box Wattie's Hash Browns
420 gram can Wattie's Baked Beans
4 eggs
4 rashers bacon
¾ cup grated Edam cheese (optional)
freshly ground black pepper to season (optional)
chopped parsley to garnish (optional)

1. Place the hash browns in the base of a 16 cm x 26 cm baking dish, trimming where necessary.
2. Pour over the baked beans and even out.
3. Beat the eggs together and pour over the top of the baked beans.
4. Finely slice the bacon and sprinkle on top of the eggs. Sprinkle over the cheese if using and season with pepper, if wished.
5. Bake at 200°C at the top of the oven for 30 minutes until set. Stand for 2 minutes before serving. Sprinkle with the chopped parsley if using. Serve in wedges.

Serves 4

Corn and bacon fritters on sweet chilli tomato

Cream-style corn has no added cream; it is the mashed corn that gives it its much-loved texture. This recipe is based on a similar recipe in the first Food in a Minute book (1997). The fritters' lovely light texture comes from the whipped egg whites. The sweet chilli tomato sauce was a modern twist, following Kiwis' new-found love of everything 'chilli'.

410 gram can Wattie's Cream Style Corn with Bacon
2 tsp minced ginger
1 small red or white onion, peeled and finely chopped
2 tblsp chopped fresh coriander or parsley
¾ cup mashed cooked cold kumara
½ cup self-raising flour
2 eggs, separated

Sweet chilli tomato sauce

1–2 spring onions, trimmed and sliced
2 tsp minced ginger
400 gram can Wattie's Sweet Chilli Style Tomatoes
1 tblsp chopped fresh coriander or parsley

1. In a bowl combine corn, ginger, onion, coriander or parsley, kumara, flour and egg yolks, mix well.
2. In a clean bowl beat the egg whites until stiff. Fold egg white carefully into corn mixture with a large metal spoon.
3. Heat a little butter or oil in a non-stick frying pan and cook large spoonfuls over a low to moderate heat for about 3 minutes each side. Keep warm in the oven until the remaining mixture is cooked.
4. In a small saucepan, gently cook the spring onions and ginger in a dash of oil for about 1 minute. Stir in tomatoes and heat gently. Season and add the coriander or parsley.
5. Serve fritters with sliced avocado and a good serving of the warm chilli sauce. Garnish with coriander, parsley or chives if wished.

Serves 5

Tropical smoothie

Milk and yoghurt are rich in calcium, vital for building strong bones. Blending milk with creamed rice, high in carbohydrates, creates a filling and nutritious snack. Great for active sports-playing kids as an after-sport snack or for a breakfast on the run.

420 gram can Wattie's Original Creamy Vanilla Creamed Rice
425 gram can Wattie's Tropical Fruit Salad in Juice, well drained
1 banana, peeled (optional)
1½ cups milk
1 cup plain or fruit salad yoghurt

1. Put the creamed rice and fruit salad chunks into a food processor or blender with the banana, if using, milk and yoghurt, and process until smooth.

2. Store in an airtight container in the fridge. Use within 3 days.

Makes 5 x 1 cup servings

Berry nice smoothie

420 gram can Wattie's Original Creamy Vanilla Creamed Rice
425 gram can Wattie's Boysenberries in Syrup, well drained
2 cups full cream milk
1 cup berry yoghurt
2 tblsp honey

1. Put the creamed rice, boysenberries, milk, yoghurt and honey into a food process or blender and process until smooth.

2. Store in an airtight container in the fridge. Use within 3 days.

Makes 5 x 1 cup servings

Salmon hash cakes

Quick and easy, these salmon hash cakes look very 'café-style' when served up in paper cases and accompanied with a salad. Ideal for weekend eating.

210 gram can Sealord Canadian Red Salmon
750 gram bag Wattie's Potatoes O'Brien Recipe Mix
3 eggs, beaten
1½–2 tsp horseradish sauce
grated rind one lemon
¼ cup chopped fresh parsley
½ cup grated cheese

1. Tip the salmon into a bowl and flake.
2. Pour the potatoes into a microwave-proof bowl, partially cover with cling film and microwave on full power (100%) for 10 minutes, stirring once during cooking.
3. In a separate bowl, beat together the eggs, horseradish, lemon rind and parsley. Season with salt and pepper. Spoon over the flaked salmon and mix with the potatoes.
4. Line 12 muffin tins with squares of baking paper. Divide salmon hash mixture evenly among the tins and press down firmly with the back of a spoon. Sprinkle each with a little grated cheese.
5. Cook at 180°C for 12–15 minutes, or until hot, set and golden. Serve with a fresh green salad and tartare sauce on the side.

Serves 4

Lunchbox roll-ups

One of our biggest areas of success on Food in a Minute is reminding families of simple ideas for children, like these roll-ups. This recipe featured on television in our second year and appeared in Food in a Minute Book 2. It remains an easy way to present a kids' favourite.

butter for spreading
sliced sandwich bread (wholemeal is best)
thinly sliced processed cheddar cheese
220 gram can Wattie's Spaghetti

1. Butter one side of a slice of bread and turn buttered side onto the board.
2. Place a slice of processed cheese on top of the unbuttered side and spread with a couple of spoonfuls of spaghetti.
3. Roll up and secure with a toothpick.
4. Bake at 190°C for about 5 minutes until crisp. Great as a hot snack or cold in the lunch-box. Remove the toothpick before serving.

Variations

- Use baked beans in place of spaghetti
- Add a slice of luncheon sausage or ham to the roll-ups, under the cheese

Makes 6–8

Asparagus slice

This rather decadent recipe was created by stylist Sarah-Jane Gillies and appeared in the third Food in a Minute book (1999). It is incredibly delicious and makes a splendid loaf to serve warm in summer with a lettuce salad on the side.

12 slices streaky bacon, rind removed
500 gram box Wattie's Potato Medallions
2 eggs
125 grams cream cheese (traditional)
½ cup cream
2 tblsp chopped dill or parsley
340 gram can Wattie's Asparagus Spears, well drained

1. Stretch the bacon rashers with the back of a large cook's knife and use them to line the base of a 25 cm x 11 cm x 7 cm loaf tin. (This is an average-sized loaf tin.)

2. Arrange the medallions in a single layer on a plate and microwave for 2 minutes to partially defrost. Cut into 1–2 cm chunks.

3. In a bowl, beat together the eggs, cream cheese, cream and dill or parsley. Fold in the chopped medallions.

4. Place one-third of the mixture in the loaf tin. Arrange half the asparagus spears on top and repeat these layers, ending with the potato mix. Fold over any bacon ends.

5. Bake at 200°C for 40 minutes. Allow to stand for 10 minutes before turning out of the tin and slicing. Serve hot or warm.

Serves 4–6

Cheat's soufflé

This easy savoury pudding makes the most of economical pantry goods. It appeared on Food in a Minute in the winter of 1999. For a change, add a well-drained can of Wattie's Asparagus Spears.

about 25 grams butter
10 slices white bread
4 rashers bacon, chopped and cooked until crisp
4 eggs
410 gram can Wattie's Cream Style Corn
2 cups milk
½ cup cheddar cheese, grated

1. Butter the bread slices and sandwich together to make 5 sandwiches. Trim the crusts from each and cut into quarters.

2. Arrange the bread randomly in a 2-litre ovenproof dish. Sprinkle over the bacon.

3. In a large bowl or jug beat together the eggs, corn and milk. Pour over the bread evenly and then sprinkle over the cheese.

4. Fan bake at 180°C (or bake at 200°C) for 30 minutes or until puffed up, golden and the centre has set. Serve hot with a crisp salad.

Serves 4–6

Crunchy fish nuggets with dips

Prepared from whole pieces of fish, these crumbed fish pieces make a quick and easy nibble. Jazz them up with one of these dips.

570 gram bag Sealord Crunchy Fish Nuggets

Creamy egg and lemon dip

- ¼ cup Eta Creamy Mayonnaise
- 2 hard-boiled eggs, peeled and diced
- ¼ cup chopped gherkins
- 1 tsp finely grated lemon rind
- 1 tblsp sliced chives

Tangy avocado dip

- ¼ cup Wattie's Bit on the Side Totally Tomato Relish
- 1 avocado, peeled and chopped
- 1 tomato, deseeded and chopped
- 1 tblsp chopped fresh basil

Creamy egg and lemon dip

Mix together the mayonnaise with the hard-boiled eggs, gherkins, lemon rind and chives and season with lemon juice, salt and pepper.

Tangy avocado dip

Mix together the tomato relish with the avocado, tomato and basil. Season with salt and pepper if needed.

1. Place the Sealord Crunchy Fish Nuggets in a single layer on a baking paper-lined oven tray.

2. Bake at 230°C for 6–7 minutes or until crunchy and hot. Serve with dips and salad greens.

Serves 4

Pizza pie

I loved this idea when it appeared back in 1998 or 1999 and still enjoy it today. Take a simple scone dough and use it to make a hearty topless pie, almost a tart, filled with your favourite pizza topping. For extra flavour add marjoram, anchovies or even sundried tomatoes.

250 gram piece mild salami, finely diced
420 gram can Wattie's Tomato and Onion Pasta Sauce.
¼ cup finely chopped stuffed olives
1 red pepper, deseeded and finely chopped (optional)
3 cups self-raising flour
50 grams butter
1½ cups grated cheddar cheese
1½ cups milk

1. Mix the salami, pasta sauce, olives and pepper together.
2. Sift the flour into a bowl and rub or cut in the butter. Stir in 1 cup of the cheese and make a well in the centre. Pour in the milk and mix to form a soft dough.
3. Turn out onto a floured board and knead lightly. Roll out to a 35–40 cm round and drape evenly over a 23 cm loose-bottom flan tin.
4. Spoon the salami filling inside. Flip over the edges (they will not completely touch) and sprinkle the remaining cheese on top.
5. Fan bake in the upper-middle section of the oven at 200°C (or bake at 220°C) for 30–35 minutes until pie is well risen, hot and golden. Serve warm.

Serves 4

Mixed bean falafels with minted yoghurt

Pulses are low in fat and salt and high in protein. Buying them canned makes it very easy to include them in your diet. In summer, cook falafels on the barbecue and enjoy with grilled vegetables such as pepper, courgettes and aubergines.

300 gram can Craig's Chickpeas in Brine, well drained
425 gram can Craig's Four Bean Mix in Brine, well drained
½ cup fresh chopped parsley
1 tblsp minced garlic
1 onion, peeled and chopped
1 tsp ground cumin
2 tsp ground coriander
3 tblsp flour
2 tblsp chopped fresh mint
½ cup Naturalea Plain Unsweetened Yoghurt

1. Put the chickpeas, beans, parsley, garlic, onion, cumin, coriander and flour into a food processor and pulse to form a smooth paste.

2. Take tablespoonful-lots of the mixture and roll into balls and flatten into patties.

3. Heat a dash of oil in a frying pan and, when hot, cook the bean patties for about 5 minutes on each side over a moderate heat until golden.

4. Mix together the mint and yoghurt and serve with falafels in bread wraps with salad ingredients.

Makes 12

Cheesy corn frittata

Wattie's created Potatoes O'Brien in 2005 and the food team were very excited by them. Small pieces of potato, peppers and onions all blanched, frozen and ready to cook made creating frittatas, chowders and savoury potato dishes incredibly easy — and it's a fabulously healthy product to keep on hand in the freezer.

4 rashers rindless bacon, thickly sliced
6 eggs
410 gram can Wattie's Cream Style Corn with Onion
6 sundried tomato halves, diced
½ cup grated cheddar or parmesan cheese
¼ cup chopped fresh parsley
750 gram bag Wattie's Potatoes O'Brien Recipe Mix
2–3 tblsp extra grated cheddar or parmesan cheese

1. Pan-fry bacon in a dash of oil until golden.
2. Beat the eggs well. Add the corn, cooked bacon, sundried tomatoes, cheese and parsley. Mix well and season with salt and pepper.
3. Cook the potatoes in a lightly oiled, large ovenproof frying pan for 5–6 minutes until hot and lightly coloured.
4. Pour in the egg mixture and cook gently over a moderate heat for 3–4 minutes. Sprinkle the top with a little extra cheese.
5. Transfer to the oven and cook at 180°C for 12–15 minutes or until golden and set. Serve with Wattie's Bit on the Side Onion Marmalade and a fresh green salad.

Serves 5–6

Winter frittata

Appearing in the winter of our first year on television, we wondered how this recipe would be received, as 10 years ago frittatas were relatively new to the café scene. This basic recipe could be jazzed up with plenty of chopped parsley or chives.

2 tblsp oil
3 potatoes, washed and evenly diced
100 grams bacon or ham, roughly diced
2 onions, peeled and finely diced
250 gram box Wattie's Frozen Chopped Spinach, defrosted and well drained
1 cup diced cheese (feta, blue or other favourites)
6 eggs

1. Heat the oil in a large ovenproof frying pan. Add the potatoes, bacon or ham, and onion and cook over a low to moderate heat for 15 minutes, stirring occasionally until the potatoes are almost cooked and very golden.

2. Arrange the spinach and cheese evenly over the pan.

3. Beat the eggs together. (You can add a pinch of salt if wished, though with feta cheese it's not a requirement.) Pour over the ingredients in the pan.

4. Cook for about 3–4 minutes on top of the stove and then transfer to a 190°C oven for about 15 minutes, until the frittata is well cooked and firm to the touch. Stand for 5 minutes before turning out to serve. Frittata is great for brunch or lunch with a large bowl of salad or steaming vegetables.

Serves 6

Chicken in pita with devilled baked beans

This recipe was filmed outdoors at our then-producer's home in 1998. Conscious of the importance of wearing hats in the sun (the campaign to prevent skin cancer was in full swing at the time) we grabbed one of Colin Follas's gardening hats and decorated it with a tea towel around the rim. I think it looked okay; the pictures of that shoot are dotted throughout the second Food in a Minute book (1998).

4 Tegel Chicken Breasts
2 tblsp Lea & Perrins Worcestershire Sauce
2 tblsp brown sugar
¼ cup water

Devilled baked beans
1 onion, peeled and chopped
1 clove garlic, crushed, peeled and mashed to a paste
420 gram can Wattie's Chunky Tomato Baked Beans
1 tblsp each wholegrain mustard, Worcestershire sauce and cider vinegar

4 large pita bread pockets
lettuce leaves for 4
2 tomatoes, diced

1. Remove the skin from the chicken breasts if wished. In a bowl mix together the Worcestershire sauce, sugar and water and add the chicken breasts. Toss to coat and leave to marinate for about 30 minutes or up to 2 hours.

2. Heat a dash of oil in a frying pan and cook the onion and garlic for about 5 minutes, until softened. Add the baked beans, mustard, Worcestershire sauce and cider vinegar and warm through.

3. Heat barbecue or frying pan and cook the chicken breasts over a moderate heat for about 20 minutes, turning once. Do not cook over too high a heat as the chicken will burn before it is cooked through.

4. Cut each breast into 3 and stuff into the centre of a pita pocket with a few lettuce leaves. Add a couple of spoonfuls of devilled baked beans and place a little chopped tomato on top.

Serves 4

Chilli Mexicana

Mince is a family household and flatter's staple. This quick and tasty chilli con carne-style recipe can be served on nachos, in tacos, in wraps or topped with pastry or potato for a quick pie.

500 grams lean beef mince
1 onion, peeled and chopped
1 tsp minced garlic
1 tsp minced red chilli
1 tsp ground cumin
420 gram can Wattie's Condensed Tomato Soup
½ cup beef stock or water
750 gram bag Wattie's Frozen Mexicana Recipe Mix
2 tblsp freshly chopped parsley or coriander

1. Quickly brown beef mince in a dash of oil in a large hot frying pan, breaking up the mince with the back of a spoon as it browns. This may be best done in two batches. Set aside.

2. Add another dash of oil to the frying pan and gently pan-fry the onion, garlic and chilli, until tender but not brown. Stir in cumin and cook for a few moments before pouring over the soup and beef stock. Cook 1–2 minutes until hot.

3. Add the Mexicana mix to the pan with the mince and heat gently, stirring until hot and tender. Season with salt, pepper and parsley or coriander. Serve Chilli Mexicana with cheesy nachos on the side.

Serves 4

Mexicana tortillas

Packed with flavour, this recipe appeared late in 2005, when Wattie's launched their Bit on the Side relishes. Foods in wraps are incredibly popular due to their 'eat anywhere' nature. Warm the tortillas to make them easier to fill and roll.

500 grams beef schnitzel, thickly sliced
1 red onion, peeled and sliced
2 tsp ground cumin
1 tsp ground coriander
3 cups Wattie's Frozen Chuckwagon Corn
300 gram can Craig's Red Kidney Beans, drained and rinsed
½ cup Wattie's Bit on the Side Sweet Chilli Jam
¼ cup chopped fresh coriander

Guacamole
1 avocado, peeled and diced
2 tomatoes, deseeded and diced
2 tblsp freshly chopped coriander
½ large mild red chilli, deseeded and chopped
2 spring onions, finely sliced

480 gram pack Quality Bakers Sundried Tomato Tortillas
lettuce for 4
sour cream to serve

1. Heat a non-stick frying pan or wok with a dash of oil and stir-fry schnitzel until just browned. This is best done in two batches. Set aside.

2. Reduce the heat and pan-fry the onion until tender, but not brown. Stir in cumin and coriander, cook for 1 minute. Increase heat and add the corn with ½ cup water and cook for 5–6 minutes or until hot and the water has almost evaporated. Add the kidney beans, browned schnitzel, chilli jam and coriander.

3. Process together the avocado, tomatoes, fresh coriander and chilli in a food processor, stir in the spring onions and season.

4. Pierce the pack of tortillas and place the whole pack in the microwave. Cook for 1 minute on high power.

5. Place some lettuce in the centre of each tortilla and pile with the hot Mexicana mix. Spoon over a little guacamole, fold to enclose the filling. Serve with sour cream on the side.

Serves 4

Quick and easy nachos

A can of corned beef can be turned into any number of dishes — all you need is a bit of creativity, as in these tasty nachos. Ideal for cooking up at the bach or having in front of the rugby in winter.

1 onion, peeled and finely chopped
425 gram can Craig's Spicy Mexican Beans
3 medium-sized tomatoes, diced
340 gram can Hellaby's Corned Beef

Topping
1 avocado, halved and stoned
1 spring onion, peeled and finely sliced
1 tblsp chopped fresh coriander or parsley
juice of 1 lemon
1 packet of nacho chips
sour cream to accompany

1. Heat a dash of oil in a frying pan and cook the onion over a gentle heat for about 5–8 minutes, or until well softened.

2. Add the Mexican beans and the tomatoes and simmer gently for 5 minutes.

3. Dice the corned beef. Add to the beans and heat through.

4. To make the topping, dice the avocado and mix with the spring onion, coriander or parsley and lemon juice.

5. Arrange a packet of your favourite nacho chips on a serving plate and spread the bean sauce on top. Top with the avocado mixture and garnish with sour cream.

Serves 4

Tex Mex tacos

This recipe is an ideal way to add healthy kidney beans to your family's diet. They come pre-cooked in the Mexicana mix and once tossed with tasty beef mince, vegetables and herbs, your family will never notice them there adding extra fibre and protein.

500 grams lean beef mince
1 onion, peeled and sliced
1 tsp minced chilli
1 tsp ground cumin
4 tblsp Wattie's Tomato Paste
400 gram can Wattie's Smoky BBQ Style Tomatoes
750 gram bag Wattie's Frozen Mexicana Recipe Mix
¼ cup fresh coriander, chopped
tacos for 4 (allow 2 per person)
lettuce for 4
½ cup grated cheese

1. Quickly brown the beef mince in a dash of oil in a hot frying pan, breaking up the mince with the back of a spoon as it browns. This is best done in two batches. Set aside.

2. Add a little more oil to the frying pan, gently cook the onion and chilli until tender, but not brown. Increase heat and add cumin and tomato paste, stirring continuously until the tomato paste starts to darken slightly, about 2 minutes.

3. Stir in the tomatoes and ¼ cup water. Return the cooked mince to the sauce, cover and simmer gently for 15 minutes.

4. Remove lid, add the Mexicana mix, stirring regularly until hot. Season with salt, pepper and coriander.

5. Heat the tacos according to the instructions on the pack. Serve crispy hot tacos, filled with lettuce, Tex Mex mince and sprinkled with cheese. Serve immediately.

Serves 4–5

Creamy pumpkin pasta, page 46

Pizza, pasta, rice, noodles & stir-fries

Italian chicken and basil pasta	42
Creamy mushroom and bacon on pasta	44
Lemon-scented dory with tomato and garlic pasta	45
Creamy pumpkin pasta	46
Easy macaroni cheese	48
Pumpkin and blue cheese fettuccine	49
Salami and feta gnocchi	50
Baked bean lasagne	52
Cheat's lasagne	53
Oriental plum pizza with hummus	54
Smoked chicken and tango chutney pizzas	55
Tomato and vegetable pizza with tuna topping	56
Tomato, smoked tuna and feta pizza	56
Lemon chicken and spinach risotto	57
Creamy mushroom risotto	58
Spinach, lemon and tuna pilaf	60
Japanese-style stir-fried beef	61
Thai-style calamari with Asian greens	62
Sweet and sour oriental pork	63

Italian chicken and basil pasta

When useful new products hit our shelves it is always great to be able to show them to you through Food in a Minute. Herbs add flavour to family cooking, giving many dishes new life and it's all the better when you can squeeze them ready-chopped from a tube!

600 grams Tegel Boneless Chicken Thigh Fillets
1 onion, peeled and chopped
1 yellow pepper, sliced
1 tsp minced garlic
3 tblsp Wattie's Tomato Paste
400 gram can Wattie's Tomatoes in Juice
¼ cup white wine or stock
400 grams dried pasta
2 tblsp Gourmet Garden Basil
¼ cup freshly grated parmesan

1. Cut each chicken thigh fillet into 4 pieces. Heat a dash of oil in a frying pan and brown the chicken pieces evenly. Set aside.

2. Gently pan-fry the onion, pepper and garlic in the residue oil, until tender, but not brown. Increase heat, stir in tomato paste, stirring continuously for 2–3 minutes or until the paste starts to darken.

3. Pour over the tomatoes in juice and white wine. Return chicken to the sauce, simmer gently for 6–8 minutes or until the chicken is cooked.

4. Cook the pasta in boiling salted water for 10–12 minutes until tender. Drain well.

5. Gently squeeze herb blend into the Italian chicken sauce, stir and season with salt and pepper if necessary. Serve over the pasta and garnish with the parmesan cheese.

Serves 4

Creamy mushroom and bacon on pasta

Pine nuts add a rich nuttiness to this sauce and while they are often seen as expensive, a few go a long way. For extra texture, add several sliced mushrooms at Step 1.

1 medium onion, peeled and finely chopped
4 rashers Kiwi bacon, finely chopped
2 tblsp oil
½ cup pine nuts
400 gram can Wattie's Creamy Mushroom and Herb Pasta Sauce
2½ –3 cups small pasta spirals
¼ cup chopped fresh herbs (parsley, basil, chives)

1. Cook the onion and bacon in the oil in a large hot frying pan until the bacon is crispy and the onion lightly browned. Add the pine nuts and cook, stirring, for a further minute until the nuts have just coloured. Set half this mixture aside.

2. Add the pasta sauce to the pan and heat through. (Or, add a dash of water to the can, swirl it around and pour into the frying pan and heat through.)

3. Cook the pasta in boiling salted water for around 12 minutes until the pasta is *al dente* (firm to the bite). Drain and add to the pan. Stir gently to coat the pasta in the mushroom sauce.

4. Serve in a bowl, topped with the remaining bacon mixture and fresh herbs for garnish.

Serves 2

Lemon-scented dory with tomato and garlic pasta

Appearing in 2005, this fish recipe was a huge success — due to its simplicity, we're sure. Vary the flavour of the sauce with other herbs such as marjoram, Italian parsley or chives.

450 gram bag Sealord Simply Natural Dory Fillets
grated rind 1 lemon
3 courgettes, trimmed and sliced
400 gram can Wattie's Chunky Tomato and Roasted Garlic Pasta Sauce
½ cup white wine or water
300 grams dried fettuccine pasta
2 tblsp chopped fresh basil leaves
¼ cup grated parmesan cheese

1. Brush dory fillets lightly with oil. Sprinkle each with a little lemon and season with black pepper.
2. Cook the fillets from frozen in a heated frying pan for about 4 minutes or until they just start to colour. Turn.
3. Scatter the courgettes around the fish and then pour over the pasta sauce and white wine or water. Cover and simmer gently for 10 minutes, or until the fish and courgettes are cooked.
4. Cook fettuccine in boiling salted water for 12 minutes or until tender. Drain well.
5. Spoon the sauce over the hot pasta and serve the fillets on top. Garnish with basil and parmesan cheese.

Serves 4

Creamy pumpkin pasta

Often the easier the ideas, the better they're received. This delicious pumpkin sauce for pasta is quickly created with a can of condensed pumpkin soup. For extra flavour and variation, add a little blue cheese or a handful of shrimps.

½ onion, peeled and finely chopped
1 tsp minced garlic
420 gram can Wattie's Condensed Creamy Pumpkin Soup
½ cup water
¼ cup grated parmesan cheese
½ cup Tararua Lite Sour Cream
2 tblsp chopped chives

1. Cook the onion and garlic in a dash of oil until the onion is soft.
2. Stir in the pumpkin soup and water and simmer for 2 minutes.
3. Add the parmesan cheese, sour cream and chives. Heat through, stirring until hot and the cheese has melted. Do not boil. Season with pepper if wished.
4. Serve over freshly cooked fettuccine or spaghetti.

Serves 3–4

Easy macaroni cheese

Celery is a wonderful vegetable to add flavour, colour and texture to family meals without too much expense. Add lots of chopped celery leaves rather than parsley for additional flavour. The leaves are great for this dish, so don't waste them.

1½ cups macaroni pasta
4 stalks celery, chopped
4 spring onions, trimmed and chopped
1 cup grated cheddar cheese
200 grams ham, diced
2–3 tblsp chopped parsley (optional)
410 gram can Wattie's Bacon & Cheese Potato Bake Sauce
1 cup milk
½ cup fresh or dried breadcrumbs (optional)

1. Cook the macaroni in boiling salted water for 10–12 minutes until *al dente* (firm to the bite). Drain and place in a bowl.

2. Stir in the celery, spring onions, half the grated cheese, ham, parsley (if using), potato bake sauce and milk. Season with pepper if wished.

3. Turn into an ovenproof dish and sprinkle over breadcrumbs and the remaining cheese.

4. Bake at 190°C for 30–35 minutes until hot and golden.

Serves 4

Pumpkin and blue cheese fettuccine

Pumpkin soup makes a great base for casseroles and pasta sauce dishes. By melting in some mellow, mild blue cheese cream cheese into this sauce, you can subtly introduce blue cheese flavours to your family.

- 400 grams dried fettuccine
- 5–6 rashers bacon, rind removed and cut into 3–4 cm pieces
- 600 grams The Good Taste Company Fresh Creamy Pumpkin Soup
- 150 gram pottle Tararua Blue Cheese and Chives Cream Cheese Spread
- 2 tblsp freshly chopped parsley or chives
- ¼ cup toasted pine nuts (optional)

1. Cook fettuccine in a large saucepan of boiling salted water until *al dente*, drain well.

2. Heat a dash of oil in a deep frying pan and quickly cook the bacon pieces until crisp and golden.

3. Stir in the soup, blue cheese and cream cheese and heat gently. Season with pepper and parsley or chives. Toss in the fettuccine and serve with toasted pine nuts, if using.

Serves 4

Salami and feta gnocchi

This simple Italian dish has all the rich flavours of the Mediterranean.

2 ½ cups milk
¾ cup semolina
1 cup grated cheddar or parmesan cheese
1 egg
¾ cup Wattie's Tomato Puree
85 gram packet Brooks Cajun Beef 90% Fat Free Salami
250 gram pottle Tararua Lite Garlic and Feta Dip

1. Bring the milk to the boil and then gradually stir in the semolina. Cook stirring for 3–4 minutes until very thick. Stir in half the grated cheese, beaten egg and season well with salt and pepper. Spoon into a baking paper-lined slice tray and refrigerate until set.

2. Spread the tomato puree into a shallow lasagne-style dish. Cut the gnocchi into squares or rounds and place into the dish, overlapping with the salami.

3. Spoon over the garlic and feta dip and then sprinkle with the remaining grated cheese.

4. Bake at 200°C for 15–20 minutes until hot and golden. Serve with seasonal vegetables.

Serves 4

Baked bean lasagne

Pumpkin has a super affinity with baked beans and it's also one of New Zealand's favourite vegetables. You could try orange-fleshed kumara for a variation. This recipe first appeared on Food in a Minute in winter 2000.

1 large onion, peeled and finely diced
2 tsp minced garlic
3–4 rashers bacon, diced (optional)
2–3 tblsp oil
820 gram can Wattie's Baked Beans
2 cups broccoli florets (optional)
2 cups mashed, cooked pumpkin

50 grams butter
4 tblsp flour
2½ cups milk
1 cup grated cheddar cheese

400 gram packet fresh lasagne

1. Cook the onion, garlic, and bacon (if using), in the oil until softened. Add the baked beans, broccoli (if using), and pumpkin and stir to mix.
2. To make the sauce layer, melt the butter in a saucepan and cook the flour for 1–2 minutes until frothy. Stir in the milk to make a smooth sauce and cook until thickened. Stir in half the cheese. Season with salt and pepper.
3. To assemble, cut the lasagne to fit an 8-cup capacity lasagne dish and place 1 layer on the bottom of the greased dish.
4. Spread over half the bean mixture and one-third of the cheese sauce. Repeat the layers, finishing with a layer of cheese sauce. Sprinkle with the remaining cheese.
5. Bake at 190°C for 45 minutes until hot and golden.

Serves 6

Cheat's lasagne

It is the times when we are challenged to create recipes from the most basic cupboard standbys that we become most creative; this recipe is a prime example. Ideal for flatters and the budget conscious.

½ small red onion, peeled and finely chopped
1 large tomato, deseeded and diced
1 tblsp freshly chopped parsley
25 grams butter
2 tblsp flour
1 cup milk
½ cup cheddar cheese, grated
2 x 400 gram cans Wattie's Pasta in Tomato and Ham Sauce
2 cups Wattie's Frozen Free Flow Spinach

1. Combine the onion, tomato and parsley. Set aside.

2. Melt the butter in a small saucepan, stir in the flour and cook until frothy. Gradually add the milk, stirring continuously until the sauce thickens. Mix in the grated cheese, reserving 2 tablespoons.

3. Spoon over one can of pasta sauce into the base of a lasagne-style dish. Sprinkle over half the onion mixture. Pour over half the hot cheese sauce, cover with an even layer of spinach. Repeat the process, finishing with the reserved cheese.

4. Microwave on high for 7–8 minutes or until hot. Alternatively cook at 180°C for 25–30 minutes until hot and golden. Serve immediately.

Serves 3–4

Oriental plum pizza with hummus

Pizzas have become one of our most loved fast meal ideas and they have been revolutionised from the classic cheese and tomato pizza into sensational taste treats. Food in a Minute has kept up with this trend, offering great healthy ideas like this pizza from 1999.

¾ cup hummus (recipe follows)
2 large pizza bases
300 gram bottle Wattie's Bit on the Side Oriental Plum Sauce
100 grams crumbled feta
1 cup grated cheddar cheese
200 grams shaved ham or 1 double breast smoked chicken, finely shredded
1 courgette, trimmed and very thinly sliced
1 red pepper, very thinly sliced

Hummus
300 gram can Craig's Chickpeas in Brine, well drained
2 tsp minced garlic
½ tsp salt
½ tsp cayenne pepper
2 tblsp oil
juice 1 lemon

1. Spread half the hummus evenly over the two pizza bases. Sprinkle liberally with the plum sauce.
2. Scatter over the feta and half the cheese.
3. Top with the ham or chicken, courgette and pepper.
4. Sprinkle over the remaining cheese and a little more plum sauce if wished.
5. Bake at 230°C at the top of the oven for 15 minutes until the pizza is piping hot. Serve immediately with the remaining hummus.

Hummus

Put all the ingredients in the food processor, fitted with a metal blade and process until smooth.

Serves 6

Smoked chicken and tango chutney pizzas

Conscious of the need to keep the fat level down in our Food in a Minute recipes, we tend to use feta cheese. However, you can use mozzarella or cheddar.

2 x 22 cm pizza bases
¾ cup hummus
16–20 fresh basil leaves
2–3 spring onions, trimmed and sliced
300 gram Tegel Smoked Breast Fillet, sliced
12 black or green olives
150 grams feta, crumbled
310 gram jar Wattie's Bit on the Side Fruit Tango Chutney

1. Brush pizza crusts lightly with olive oil. Spread pizza bases evenly with hummus, sprinkle over basil leaves and spring onions.
2. Arrange slices of chicken on top with olives and crumble over feta.
3. Cook at 220°C for 8–10 minutes until golden and cooked through.
4. Place small spoonfuls of chutney evenly over the pizzas. Serve immediately with a tossed green salad.

Serves 5–6

Tomato and vegetable pizza with tuna topping

Lemon and basil add zest to canned tuna, creating a pizza with lots of flavour.

22 cm pizza base
150 gram pouch Wattie's Very Special Tomato and Fresh Basil Pasta Sauce
½ cup grated mozzarella cheese
½ red pepper, sliced
1 small courgette, trimmed and peeled into thin strips
1 small avocado, peeled and diced
2 spring onions, trimmed and finely sliced
1 tblsp fresh lime or lemon juice
grated rind ½ lemon
1 tblsp chopped fresh basil or parsley
95 gram can Greenseas Smoke Flavoured Tuna, drained

1. Spread the pizza base with the pasta sauce. Sprinkle over the mozzarella, red pepper and courgette.
2. Bake at 220°C for 8–10 minutes until golden and cooked through.
3. Toss together the avocado, spring onions, lime or lemon juice, lemon rind, basil or parsley and tuna. Sprinkle over hot pizza and serve.

Serves 2–3

Tomato, smoked tuna and feta pizza

With pizza bases so readily available in supermarkets, making pizzas has become so much easier. Toppings can be as varied as you wish — the healthier, the better.

22 cm pizza base
150 gram pouch Wattie's Very Special Tomato and Fresh Basil Pasta Sauce
about 12 fresh basil leaves
½ red onion, peeled and finely sliced
75 grams feta, crumbled
95 gram can Greenseas Smoke Flavoured Tuna, drained
8 black olives

1. Spread the pizza base with the pasta sauce.
2. Sprinkle over the basil leaves, red onion and feta. Flake the tuna evenly onto the pizza and top with olives.
3. Bake at 220°C for 8–10 minutes until golden and hot.

Serves 2–3

Lemon chicken and spinach risotto

Over the years Food in a Minute has kept up with the trends, adding recipes such as risotto to our repertoire. This quick and easy version of a classic risotto has a lovely creamy finish and a fresh flavour with the addition of rosemary.

- 1 onion, peeled and chopped
- 1 tsp minced garlic
- 4 boneless Tegel Chicken Thigh Fillets, diced
- 2 cups arborio rice or short grain rice
- 420 gram can Wattie's Condensed Creamy Chicken Soup
- grated rind and juice 2 lemons
- 4 cups chicken stock
- 350 gram bag Wattie's Frozen Free Flow Spinach
- 2 tblsp freshly chopped rosemary

1. Heat a little oil in a large lidded saucepan. Add onion, garlic and chicken and cook over a moderately high heat for 3–5 minutes, until the chicken is browned and the onion and garlic have softened.

2. Add the rice and toss to coat in the onion. Add the soup, lemon rind, juice and chicken stock. Stir to mix well.

3. Cover and simmer very gently for 20–25 minutes, stirring occasionally until the rice is tender and all liquid has almost been absorbed.

4. Lightly stir in the spinach and rosemary and cook for a further 2–3 minutes or until the spinach is hot. Serve immediately.

Serves 4–5

Creamy mushroom risotto

When Food in a Minute began, risottos were not commonplace, nowadays they're on all the café menus and popular at home too. I like to add extra chopped mushrooms to the recipe for additional colour, texture and flavour. Try sliced Swiss browns and button mushrooms.

25 grams butter
1 onion, peeled and finely chopped
2 tsp minced garlic
2 cups short grain rice
1 cup dry white wine
3½ cups chicken stock
420 gram can Wattie's Condensed Creamy Mushroom Soup
½ cup grated parmesan cheese
¼ cup cream

1. Heat the butter in a large saucepan, add the onion and cook over a moderately low heat for 8–10 minutes until very soft but not coloured. Add the garlic and cook a further minute.

2. Add the rice and stir in the butter and onion mixture until the rice begins to change to a white colour.

3. Add the wine and stir constantly over a moderately low heat until the rice has absorbed all the wine.

4. Add the chicken stock to the risotto, ½ cup at a time, stirring continuously. When each amount has been absorbed add the next measure.

5. When all the stock has been added, stir in the mushroom soup and continue to stir over a low heat until the risotto is thick and creamy.

6. Stir in the parmesan cheese and cream and season with salt and pepper. Serve over grilled mushrooms and crispy bacon rashers with chopped parsley to garnish.

Serves 4

Spinach, lemon and tuna pilaf

When Wattie's introduced its Oriental Recipe Mix to the market, it allowed us to create easy pilafs and stir-fries, making nutritious meals in minutes. For a better flavour use a fragrant Indian curry paste.

1 small onion, chopped
1 tsp minced garlic
1 tblsp curry powder or paste
½ x 750 gram bag Wattie's Frozen Oriental Recipe Mix
1 tsp finely grated lemon rind
1 cup Wattie's Frozen Free Flow Spinach
95 gram can Greenseas 98% Fat Free Oven Dried Tomato and Onion Tuna
¼ cup toasted almonds or cashew nuts

1. Heat a dash of oil in a frying pan and cook the onion and garlic over a medium heat until softened. Stir in the curry powder or paste and cook a further minute.

2. Add rice 'n veges mix, lemon rind and a pinch of salt. Pan-fry for 3–4 minutes.

3. Stir in the spinach and cook until the spinach is just heated through.

4. Gently flake in the tuna. Serve immediately garnished with almonds or cashew nuts.

Serves 2–3

Japanese-style stir-fried beef

Of all the brands that Wattie's market, Lea & Perrins classic Worcestershire sauce is one of my favourites. Somehow though, over the last few years, it seems to have been pushed to the back of the cupboard as chilli sauces have become so popular. It is fabulous in some Japanese dishes such as this one, so bring it back to the front of the cupboard and use it to add flavour to casseroles, soups and sauces.

600 grams rump steak
1 tblsp minced ginger
1 tblsp sweet chilli sauce
¼ cup sherry
¼ cup Lea & Perrins Worcestershire Sauce
250 grams Swiss brown mushrooms, wiped and thickly sliced
1 red pepper, thickly sliced
200 grams green beans, trimmed and halved lengthwise
1 bunch spring onions, cut into 5 cm lengths
270 gram pack dried udon noodles
½ cup beef stock
1 tsp cornflour

1. Cut the rump steak into thin strips and place in a snaplock bag with ginger, sweet chilli sauce, sherry and Worcestershire sauce. Seal bag and toss to coat evenly, refrigerate for 10–15 minutes. Drain beef, reserving marinade.

2. Heat a dash of oil in a hot frying pan or wok, stir-fry beef strips until browned, set aside.

3. Add a little more oil to the frying pan and stir-fry the mushrooms, pepper, beans and spring onions until crisp and tender.

4. Cook udon noodles according to the directions on the pack.

5. Return meat to the frying pan. Mix together reserved marinade, beef stock and cornflour, pour into stir-fry, toss quickly and cook until the sauce thickens. Serve over cooked udon noodles.

Serves 4

Thai-style calamari with Asian greens

From time to time we have 10 sponsors on Food in a Minute and lately we have welcomed Sealord onto the show. Their frozen products are good quality and ideal to keep on hand in busy households. This calamari stir-fry appeared just recently in 2006.

400 gram bag Wattie's Wok Creations Frozen Asian Greens Stir Fry Vegetables
1 tblsp shredded ginger
340 gram bag Sealord Tender Calamari Rings with Thai Style Mild Chilli Dipping Sauce
1 tblsp freshly chopped coriander
1 tblsp toasted sesame seeds

1. Thaw the calamari rings and dipping sauce. Pat the calamari dry or drain off the liquid.

2. Heat a large deep non-stick frying pan or wok with a dash of oil and stir-fry ginger for 1 minute. Add stir-fry vegetables, toss with ginger and stir-fry for 4–5 minutes until hot. Set aside.

3. Add more oil if needed to the frying pan and cook the calamari rings for 2–3 minutes or until just cooked through.

4. Drizzle over the dipping sauce and return the stir-fried vegetables to the pan and toss together. Sprinkle with coriander and sesame seeds. Serve over noodles or rice.

Serves 2

Sweet and sour oriental pork

Sweet and sour is probably New Zealand's favourite Chinese-style sauce, as each time we put a sweet and sour meal to air, it is incredibly popular — especially when they are this easy.

600 grams 100% New Zealand Trim Pork Leg Steaks, sliced
1 tblsp minced ginger
1 bunch spring onions, trimmed and sliced
750 gram bag Wattie's Frozen Oriental Recipe Mix
425 gram can Wattie's Stir Fry Sweet & Sour Sauce
¼ cup toasted cashew nuts

1. Heat a large non-stick frying pan or wok with a dash of oil and stir-fry pork strips, this may be best done in two batches. Set aside.

2. Add a second dash of oil to the frying pan and stir-fry ginger and spring onions for 2–3 minutes. Add the oriental mix and stir-fry for a further 4 minutes, tossing continuously until hot.

3. Pour over sweet and sour sauce and about ¼ cup water. Stir to combine then reduce heat and simmer for 4 minutes or until piping hot. Gently mix in the browned pork strips and heat through. Serve in bowls, garnished with toasted cashew nuts.

Serves 4

Cumin and lemon baked chicken, page 84

Bakes, braises & pies

Chickpea and pumpkin casserole	68
Country French meatballs	69
Beef and bean casserole	70
French country casserole	72
Herbed porcupines	73
Made-in-one-pan dinner	74
Moroccan-style beef and beans	75
Tasty all-in-one meatballs	76
Tasty beef bolognese	77
Winter beef casserole	78
Chicken in a pot	80
Chicken with mustard crème fraîche sauce	81
Creamy sundried tomato stuffed chicken breasts	82
Easy chicken vegetable bake	83
Cumin and lemon baked chicken	84
Malay chicken satay on oriental rice	86
Sweet and sour chicken	87
Tuscan chicken	88
Country lamb casserole	89
Hearty lamb shanks	90
Lamb provençale	91
Moroccan lamb	92
Moroccan lamb pilaf	93

Tuscan lamb shanks	94
Boston baked beans	95
Golden plum pork loin chops	96
Macaroni cheese bake	97
Spanish pork chops with Mediterranean vegetable roasters	98
Sweet apple and pork braise	99
Autumn sausages	100
Fruity devilled sausages	101
Sausage hot pot	102
Winter sausages	104
Spinach and feta filo pie	106
Flamenco pie	107
French beef and mushroom cottage pie	108
Chicken and spinach pies	109
Cranberry and chicken pie	110
Creamy chicken and corn pie	112
Creamy smoked chicken filo pie	113
Pumpkin and chicken pie	114
Winter chicken pie	115
Smoked fish pie with garlic bread crust	116

Sausage hot pot, page 102

Chickpea and pumpkin casserole

If there's only vegetables in the fridge, then this casserole could be just the thing. Add a handful of chopped herbs such as marjoram, parsley or chives for extra flavour.

1 onion, peeled and finely chopped
1 tblsp minced garlic
1 tblsp paprika
500–600 grams pumpkin, peeled
300 gram can Craig's Chickpeas in Brine, well drained
400 gram can Wattie's Tomatoes in Juice, diced
½ cup raisins
1 cup vegetable stock or water
12 Brussels sprouts, trimmed and halved, or 2 cups broccoli florets
salt and pepper to taste

1. Heat a dash of oil in a flame-proof casserole or lidded frying pan. Add the onion and cook for 3–5 minutes until soft.
2. Add the garlic and paprika and cook for a further minute.
3. Cut the pumpkin into 2 cm pieces and add to the pan with the chickpeas, tomatoes, raisins and stock or water. Cover and simmer for 10 minutes.
4. Add the Brussels sprouts or broccoli to the casserole, cover and simmer for a further 5 minutes or until the vegetables are tender. Season with salt and pepper before serving over rice.

Serves 4

Country French meatballs

When pan-frying meatballs, make sure you have the pan hot to seal and brown the meatballs without them sticking to the pan. For more spice, add a good pinch of cayenne pepper or chilli powder to the meatballs.

250–350 grams beef mince
250 grams sausage meat
2–4 tblsp chopped fresh parsley or 1 tblsp dried parsley
1 tsp dried mixed herbs
2 tsp prepared mustard
1 onion, peeled and sliced, or use a leek if preferred
250 grams flat mushrooms, sliced
545 gram can Wattie's Just Add Country French Mince Simmer Sauce
½ cup beef stock or water

1. In a bowl mix together the beef mince, sausage meat, herbs and mustard and season with salt and pepper. Use wet hands to roll the mixture into 14–16 balls.

2. Heat a dash of oil in a lidded frying pan and quickly brown the meatballs and sliced onion or leek.

3. Add the mushrooms, simmer sauce and beef stock or water. Stir to mix.

4. Cover and simmer for 30 minutes or until piping hot and the meatballs are cooked. Scatter with chopped parsley before serving if wished.

Serves 4–5

Beef and bean casserole

For a deep mushroom flavour use Portobello mushrooms or fresh field mushrooms.

500 grams Quality Mark Lean Chuck Steak
dash of oil
2 onions, peeled and cut into 2 cm dice
1 tblsp paprika
400 gram can Wattie's Whole Peeled Tomatoes in Juice
425 gram can Craig's Spicy Mexican Beans
about 12 mushrooms, diced
½ cup beef stock or water

1. Cut the chuck steak into large, 3 cm pieces.
2. Heat the oil in a frying pan and brown the meat over a moderate to high heat, then transfer to a casserole. This is best done in two batches.
3. Add the onion to the pan and cook for 2–3 minutes. Sprinkle over the paprika and cook for ½ minute before stirring in the tomatoes, beans, mushrooms and beef stock or water.
4. Bring the mixture to the boil and then pour over the beef. Cover and cook at 160°C for 1¼ hours until the meat is tender.
5. Serve hot with your favourite green vegetable.

Serves 4

French country casserole

I am a great fan of hearty casseroles. There's only a little prep work involved, and cooking is completed without having to watch over the dish. Along with this, you can add plenty of vegetables to accompany the meat and make a hearty meal. Serve as is, or with a simple crispy sliced bread and cheese topping. This basic recipe first appeared around 1997 or 1998 and we have made a number of variations over the years. Use other casserole cuts of beef, if you wish.

750 grams lean cross-cut blade steak
1 leek, trimmed and washed
2 carrots, peeled and trimmed
545 gram can Wattie's Just Add Country French Mince Simmer Sauce
about 12–16 large flat mushrooms, quartered
1 cup Wattie's Frozen Minted Baby Peas
about 12 slices French bread
1 cup cheddar grated cheese

1. Cut the meat into 3 cm pieces
2. Heat a dash of oil in an ovenproof casserole and brown the meat on all sides over a high heat.
3. Chop the leek and carrots and add to the casserole with the simmer sauce and the mushrooms.
4. Cook at 180°C for 1¼ hours or until the meat is tender.
5. Stir through the minted baby peas. Arrange the French bread slices in an overlapping layer around the outside.
6. Sprinkle the cheese over the bread slices. Fan grill for about 8–10 minutes until the bread slices are golden.
7. Serve with mashed potatoes.

Serves 4–6

Herbed porcupines

A favourite from the early years of Food in a Minute. Adding rice to mince meatballs will add texture and fibre, as well as helping to stretch the meat content. For a change, use a can of Wattie's Condensed Tomato Soup in place of the simmer sauce.

500 grams Quality Mark Lean Minced Beef
½ cup uncooked, long grain rice
¼ cup chopped fresh herbs, like thyme or parsley
salt and pepper to season
1 tblsp oil
1 onion, peeled and finely sliced
2 carrots, peeled and finely chopped
550 gram can Wattie's Just Add Hearty Savoury Mince Simmer Sauce
2 cups water

1. In a bowl mix together the minced beef, rice and herbs and season with salt and pepper.
2. Roll into 12–14 even-shaped balls.
3. Heat the oil in a frying pan and add the onion and carrot. Cook for 3–4 minutes until just softened. Add the simmer sauce and water and bring to the boil.
4. Add the meatballs and cover. Simmer gently for 30 minutes, turning once during the cooking time. Serve garnished with a little chopped fresh herb and your favourite seasonal vegetables.

Serves 4–6

Made-in-one-pan dinner

This good old-fashioned but incredibly useful recipe appeared in Food in a Minute Book 3. Yeast-based spreads and Wattie's Tomato Sauce are great to add flavour to a basic mince dish and most of us have these in our cupboards. Add mixed vegetables in place of the corn, if you wish.

1 onion, peeled and diced
500 grams Quality Mark Lean Minced Beef
2 tblsp oil
1 large golden kumara, peeled and diced
2 tsp Marmite, Vegemite or Promite
1 tblsp flour
½ cup Wattie's Tomato Sauce
1½ cups water
½ x 750 gram bag Wattie's Frozen Chuckwagon Corn

1. Cook the onion and mince in the oil in a large, lidded frying pan over a high heat for 4–5 minutes, until the onion has softened and the mince has browned. Break up the mince with the back of a wooden spoon or a fork as you go. It is best to do this in two batches, otherwise the mince will stew rather than brown. Stir in the kumara.

2. In a jug, mix together the Marmite, flour, tomato sauce and water and pour over the mince. Cover and simmer gently for 10–15 minutes until the kumara is almost cooked.

3. Add the corn mix and stir. Cover and simmer for a further 10 minutes. Season with salt and pepper if wished.

Serves 4

Moroccan-style beef and beans

Lemon can be used in both sweet and savoury dishes and it's particularly delicious in this Moroccan-inspired dish.

500 grams beef mince
1 onion, peeled and chopped
1–2 stalks celery, sliced
400 gram can Wattie's Moroccan Style Tomatoes
420 gram can Wattie's Mild Chilli Beans
1 tblsp freshly chopped thyme

Crispy Crumb Topping

2 cups fresh breadcrumbs
1 tblsp freshly chopped thyme
1 tsp minced garlic
2 tsp finely grated lemon rind
2 tblsp oil or butter, melted

1. Quickly brown the beef mince in a dash of oil in a hot frying pan, breaking up the mince with the back of a spoon as it browns. (This may be best done in two batches.) Set aside.

2. Gently fry onion and celery in the residue oil, until tender, but not brown. Pour over tomatoes and chilli beans and add browned mince. Heat gently and season with thyme, salt and pepper. Simmer gently for 6–8 minutes.

3. Toss breadcrumbs, thyme, garlic, lemon rind and oil or butter together, season with salt and pepper.

4. Spoon hot tomato and bean mixture into an ovenproof serving dish, scatter over the crumb topping. Bake at 200°C for 20 minutes. Serve immediately.

Serves 4–6

Tasty all-in-one meatballs

Beef mince is a weekly mainstay in many New Zealand homes, so whenever we prepare a recipe with beef mince, we can count on it being a huge success. On this occasion, paired up with tomato sauce, we had a real winner on our hands.

- 1 onion, peeled and chopped
- 200 grams flat mushrooms, wiped and chopped
- 500 grams lean beef mince
- ½ cup dried breadcrumbs
- 2 tblsp freshly chopped parsley
- 1 egg, beaten
- ¼ cup Lea & Perrins Worcestershire Sauce
- 1 leek, washed and sliced
- ¾ cup orzo pasta
- 420 gram can Wattie's Condensed Tomato Soup
- 1½ cups beef stock
- 1 cup water

1. Pan-fry the onion in a dash of oil until just beginning to soften. Increase heat, add mushrooms and cook, stirring, until tender. Cool.

2. In a bowl combine beef mince, breadcrumbs, parsley, cooked onion and mushrooms, egg and Worcestershire sauce, mix well. With wet hands roll mixture into small balls.

3. Heat a deep-lidded frying pan with a dash of oil and brown the meatballs. Scatter over the leek and orzo pasta. Pour in the soup, stock, water and season with salt and pepper. Stir to mix.

4. Cover and simmer very gently for 25 minutes, or until the meatballs and orzo are tender. Garnish with extra parsley if wished.

Serves 4–5

Tasty beef bolognese

A quick and easy take on a family favourite.

- 1 onion, peeled and diced
- 1 tsp minced garlic
- 1 red pepper, deseeded and thickly sliced
- 3 tblsp Wattie's Tomato Paste
- 400 gram can Wattie's Whole Peeled Tomatoes in Juice
- ¼ cup water
- 1 tblsp chopped fresh parsley
- 340 gram can Hellaby's Corned Beef, or Hellaby's Reduced Fat Corned Beef, chilled

1. Gently cook the onion, garlic and pepper in a dash of oil until tender, but not brown.
2. Increase the heat and add the tomato paste, cook stirring for 2 minutes. Add the tomatoes and water. Mix well and season with parsley and pepper.
3. Cut the corned beef into 2 cm pieces and fold into the tomato sauce, heat gently and serve over your favourite pasta.

Serves 3–4

Winter beef casserole

A fabulously versatile, classic Food in a Minute casserole recipe. Cross-cut beef is my favourite cut for casseroles, though others include gravy beef and chuck steak or, for a change, use diced shoulder of lamb.

750 grams cross-cut beef
2 tblsp seasoned flour
2–3 tblsp oil
½ cup Wattie's Tomato Sauce
2 tblsp Lea & Perrins Worcestershire Sauce
1½ cups beef stock
2 onions, peeled and roughly cut
2 stalks celery, trimmed and chopped
1 carrot, peeled and diced
250 grams mushrooms, halved
chopped parsley to serve

1. Trim the meat of any extra fat and cut into large 3 cm pieces.

2. Toss the meat in the seasoned flour.

3. Heat the oil in a frying pan and cook the meat over a high heat until it is well browned on all sides. Transfer to a casserole. Blend together the remaining seasoned flour with the tomato sauce, Worcestershire sauce and beef stock. Pour into the pan and bring to the boil. Transfer to the casserole.

4. Add the onions, celery, carrots and mushrooms to the pan and cook 3–4 minutes.

5. Cook on top of the stove for 1¼ –1½ hours or in a 180°C oven for the same time. Season with pepper and chopped parsley and serve with plenty of mashed potatoes and Brussels sprouts or your favourite green vegetable.

Serves 4

Top: Winter beef casserole
Bottom: French beef and mushroom cottage pie, page 108

Chicken in a pot

Another one of our successful one-pot meal ideas. Serve up with a pile of your favourite greens.

4 tblsp oil
1 onion, peeled and chopped
2 stalks celery, trimmed and chopped
500 gram bag Wattie's Frozen Baby Carrots
6–8 pieces Tegel Boneless Chicken Thighs
550 gram can Wattie's Just Add Curry Mince Simmer Sauce
2 potatoes, well scrubbed, not peeled

1. Heat half the oil in a large frying pan and quickly brown the onion and celery. Transfer to a large, 3-litre capacity casserole.
2. Sprinkle the frozen carrots over the vegetables.
3. Return the pan to the heat and add the remaining oil. Quickly brown the chicken thighs over a high heat.
4. Arrange the chicken thighs on top of the vegetables. Pour the simmer sauce evenly over the top.
5. Cut the potatoes into thin slices and overlap evenly over the top.
6. Cover and cook at 180°C for 1¼ hours until the potatoes are tender and the chicken cooked.

Serves 4–6

Chicken with mustard crème fraîche sauce

One of our long-standing partners on Food in a Minute is Mainland Foods who sell Tararua creams, desserts and cheeses. Crème fraîche is a thick, slightly tangy, fresh cream that will not separate when heated to boiling point, making it ideal for quick pan sauces such as this one.

2 tblsp oil or butter
4 medium (150 grams) Tegel Tenderbasted Chicken Breasts
1½ cups mushrooms, sliced
1 onion, peeled and finely chopped
1 tblsp French or Dijon prepared mustard
250 gram pottle Tararua Crème Fraîche

1. Heat half the oil or butter in a frying pan and when hot, place the chicken breasts skin side down first. Cover with a lid and cook over a moderate heat for 5 minutes.
2. Turn over and cook a further 5–7 minutes or until the chicken is cooked. Set aside on a plate and keep covered.
3. Add the remaining oil or butter to the pan and when hot, stir in the mushrooms and onion and cook over a moderate heat, stirring regularly until the vegetables are softened.
4. Stir in the mustard and crème fraîche and bring to a gentle simmer. Return the chicken to the pan, cover and heat through for a further 1–2 minutes. Season well with salt and pepper. Serve with vegetables.

Serves 4

Creamy sundried tomato stuffed chicken breasts

Co-sponsor Mainland launched their Sundried Tomato Cream Cheese Spread on Food in a Minute in 2004, giving us a chance to do something a wee bit special.

4 Tegel Fresh Chicken Skinless Single Breast Fillets
150 gram pottle Tararua Sundried Tomato Cream Cheese Spread
1 cup baby spinach leaves
1 onion, peeled and chopped
400 gram can Wattie's Chopped Tomatoes with Green Capsicum
½ cup white wine, chicken stock or water
chopped fresh basil and grated parmesan cheese to garnish

1. Cut a small pocket in the thick side of each chicken breast. Spread an equal amount of cream cheese into each pocket. Divide spinach leaves evenly among the chicken. Secure the openings with toothpicks.

2. Pan-fry the chicken breast in a moderately hot, lightly oiled lidded frying pan for 4 minutes each side. Set aside.

3. Add the onion to the pan and cook until tender. Stir in the tomatoes and wine or stock. Return the chicken to the frying pan, cover and simmer gently for 20–25 minutes or until tender and well cooked. Garnish with the basil and grated parmesan cheese and serve with pasta if wished.

Serves 4–5

Easy chicken vegetable bake

Wattie's Condensed Creamy Chicken Soup makes an easy base for casseroles. For an additional creamy texture, stir in half a cup of sour cream with the soup.

2 large potatoes, peeled and finely sliced
500 grams boneless chicken thighs, diced
1 onion, peeled and finely diced
1 cup grated pumpkin or carrot
2–3 cups mixed fresh vegetables
420 gram can Wattie's Condensed Creamy Chicken Soup
2 tblsp chopped parsley
¼ cup each fresh breadcrumbs and grated cheese

1. Place the sliced potatoes in an overlapping layer in the base of a lasagne-style dish.
2. In a bowl mix together the chicken, onion, grated pumpkin or carrot, vegetables, soup and parsley.
3. Spread the mixture evenly over the sliced potatoes. Sprinkle with the breadcrumbs and cheese.
4. Bake at 180°C for 40–45 minutes until golden and hot.

Serves 4

Cumin and lemon baked chicken

At the beginning of 2006 we were joined by Gregg's on Food in a Minute, allowing us to offer up this tasty idea for autumn.

1 red onion, peeled and sliced
3 courgettes, wiped and sliced
1 green pepper, sliced
400 gram can Wattie's Sweet Chilli Style Tomatoes
½ cup chicken stock, water or white wine
35 gram jar Gregg's Spiced Cumin & Lemon Seasoning
4 Tegel Chicken Leg And Thigh Portions, trim any excess fat
1 tblsp freshly chopped coriander or parsley to garnish

1. Layer the red onion, courgettes and green pepper in a lasagne-style dish.

2. Spoon over chilli tomatoes and chicken stock.

3. Tip the cumin and lemon seasoning into a plastic bag. Add the chicken portions and toss to coat in the seasoning mix.

4. Arrange the chicken over the vegetables and tomatoes.

5. Bake at 200°C for about 45 minutes or until the chicken is golden and cooked through. Garnish with the coriander and serve with rice or couscous.

Serves 4

Malay chicken satay on oriental rice

There is something deliciously more-ish about coconut, peanuts and chicken as a combination. These satays are super cooked on the barbecue.

210 gram pouch Wattie's Wok Creations Malaysian Peanut Satay Stir Fry Sauce
½ tsp finely grated lime rind
2 tblsp fresh lime juice
500 grams Tegel Chicken Tenderloins or Boneless Chicken Breast Fillets, cut into 2–3 cm strips
1 tblsp shredded ginger
750 gram bag Wattie's Frozen Oriental Recipe Mix
½ cup coconut milk
½ cup roasted peanuts
1 tblsp freshly chopped coriander

1. Combine ¼ cup satay sauce with lime rind and juice in a medium snaplock bag and marinate chicken for 15–20 minutes.

2. Thread chicken onto pre-soaked bamboo skewers, reserve marinade. Barbecue over a medium heat for 4–5 minutes each side, until golden and cooked through.

3. In a wok or large deep frying pan, cook the ginger in a dash of oil until tender. Add Oriental mix with ¼ cup water and stir-fry for 5–7 minutes or until the vegetables are hot.

4. Combine reserved marinade, remaining satay sauce with coconut milk in a small saucepan, bring to the boil, reduce heat and simmer for 2–3 minutes.

5. Serve chicken satays on cooked oriental mix, spoon over sauce and garnish with roasted peanuts and coriander.

Serves 4

Sweet and sour chicken

When stir-frying frozen vegetables, have the wok or frying pan very very hot and keep the heat high to ensure they stir-fry as opposed to steaming. For coriander lovers, add a small handful of freshly chopped leaves to the sauce and garnish with toasted cashew nuts.

1 egg yolk
¾ cup iced water
1 cup flour, sifted
1–2 tblsp oil
1 onion, peeled and diced
3–4 cups Wattie's Frozen Stir Fry Vegetable Mix
425 gram can Wattie's Stir Fry Sweet & Sour Sauce
1 cup oil for shallow frying
450 grams Tegel Chicken Breast Stir Fry

1. Prepare the batter by mixing the egg yolk and water together and then quickly beating in the flour. Stand for 30 minutes.

2. Heat the first measure of oil in a frying pan or wok and quickly cook the onion over a high heat for 2 minutes. Stir in the frozen vegetables and cook for a further 2 minutes. Add the sweet and sour sauce and heat through. Keep warm.

3. Heat enough oil in a wok or deep frying pan for shallow frying. Dip the chicken pieces into the batter and cook in the hot oil for about 3–5 minutes until golden and crispy. Lift out with a slotted spoon. Drain on absorbent paper.

4. Serve the chicken piled high in a bowl and spoon the sweet and sour vegetables on top.

Serves 4

Tuscan chicken

This recipe was mocked up and presented to Wattie's back in 1996 to show them the concept of Food in a Minute. This rest is history.

8 Tegel Chicken Drumsticks
1 tblsp flour
2 tblsp oil
2 onions, peeled and sliced
about 2 cups mushrooms, halved
400 gram can Wattie's Italian Style Tomatoes
12 stuffed green olives
plenty freshly ground black pepper
pasta for 4 to accompany (shape of your choice)
Wattie's Frozen Whole Baby Beans to accompany

1. Remove the skin from the drumsticks if wished. (It will help us trim excess fat from the meal.) Put the flour into a bag and toss the chicken legs in the flour.
2. Heat the oil in a large lidded non-stick frying pan.
3. Add the chicken pieces and brown over a moderately high heat for 10 minutes, turning regularly so that the chicken browns evenly.
4. Add the onions, mushrooms, tomatoes, olives and season well with freshly ground black pepper.
5. Cover and simmer over a low heat for 20 minutes.
6. Serve with the beans and hot, freshly cooked pasta tossed with a little butter and fresh herbs.

Serves 4

Country lamb casserole

This recipe was based loosely on the idea of an Irish stew. We wanted to make an easy one-pot winter meal with new products: the Stock Pot Vegetable soup mix and the Frozen Winter Vegetables Recipe Mix. The final recipe is delicious, served on a cool autumn or winter's night with toasted crusty bread.

8–10 lamb shoulder chops, trimmed
1 large onion, peeled and sliced
2 tsp minced garlic
2 bay leaves
210 gram pack Wattie's Stock Pot Vegetable
6 cups boiling water
750 gram bag Wattie's Frozen Winter Vegetables Recipe Mix
Lea & Perrins Worcestershire sauce
2 tblsp freshly chopped parsley

1. Cut lamb shoulder chops in half lengthwise. Brown the chops in a hot frying pan, with a dash of oil, turning once.

2. Layer the browned lamb, onion, garlic and bay leaves in a deep casserole or saucepan, sprinkle over the stock pot vegetables, pour over boiling water. Cover and simmer gently on top of the stove or cook in the oven at 170°C for 1¼ hours, or until the lamb is tender.

3. Add the winter vegetables, cook for a further 5–8 minutes or until hot and cooked through, season with salt and pepper and Lea & Perrins Worcestershire Sauce. Remove bay leaves before serving. Serve in wide bowls garnished with the parsley.

Serves 4–6

Hearty lamb shanks

Without fail, every time lamb shanks have appeared on Food in a Minute, we have single-handedly sold the country out of shanks. Seems some old classics just keep on being favourites. For a variation use diced casserole lamb or beef in place of the shanks, cut into 3 cm pieces. Allow about 500 grams and cook for about 1¼ hours.

4–6 lamb shanks, trimmed of end knuckle
1 large onion, peeled and chopped
2 tsp minced garlic
2 parsnips, quartered lengthways
3 sticks celery, cut into 1 cm slices
2 tblsp tomato paste
1 tblsp finely grated orange rind
¾ cup orange juice
2 cups beef stock
2 bay leaves
1–2 tblsp freshly chopped thyme
¼ cup Lea & Perrins Worcestershire Sauce
600 gram bag Wattie's Frozen Traditional Vegetable Roasters

1. Heat a dash of oil in a frying pan and brown the shanks on all sides. Transfer to a casserole dish.
2. Cook onion, garlic, parsnips and celery in the remaining oil until just beginning to soften. Add the tomato paste and cook stirring for 2–3 minutes. Stir in orange rind and juice, beef stock and bay leaves.
3. Cover and cook at 160°C for 1¾ hours or until shanks are tender.
4. Remove from oven, increase oven temperature to 230°C and arrange the vegetable roasters on a baking tray. Cook for 20 minutes.
5. To finish the casserole add the Worcestershire sauce and thyme to the shanks and season with salt and pepper. Serve shanks and crispy vegetable roasters in bowls.

Serves 4–6

Lamb provençale

Lamb shoulder chops simmered gently in this tasty mixture become flavoursome and tender. When using celery I like to add the leaves as they provide a lovely fresh flavour. If you have celery seeds, add ½ tsp to this recipe — they'll add another layer of flavour.

- 4–6 lamb shoulder steaks or chops
- 1 tblsp oil
- 1 onion, peeled and finely diced
- 2 stalks celery, trimmed and finely diced
- 400 gram can Wattie's Tomato and Herb Pasta Sauce
- ½ cup water
- 300 gram can Craig's Mixed Beans in Brine, well drained
- ¼ cup chopped celery leaves to garnish
- 12 olives (black or stuffed), optional

1. Trim any excess fat from the lamb steaks or chops.
2. Heat the oil in a lidded frying pan and brown the chops evenly on both sides. Add the onion, celery, tomato and herb pasta sauce, water and the mixed beans. Cover and simmer gently for 40 minutes.
3. Add the celery leaves and olives, if using, 5 minutes before end of cooking time.
4. Serve with vegetables and potato pom poms in garlic butter.

Pom Poms in Garlic Butter

Cook Wattie's Potato Pom Poms in the oven according to the directions on the back of the packet. Heat 2 tblsp garlic butter in a frying pan and toss the pom poms in the hot garlic butter before serving.

Serves 4

Moroccan lamb

Meat cooked in a sauce or casserole still needs to rest before serving. This way it will be tender and juicy to eat. Allow about 10 minutes to rest, once removed from the heat, before serving.

500 grams diced shoulder lamb
2 onions, peeled and roughly chopped
1 green or red pepper, deseeded and chopped
½ cup raisins or chopped dried apricots
400 gram can Wattie's Moroccan Style Tomatoes
½ cup water or beef stock

Cous cous
1½ cups boiling water or chicken stock
1 cup couscous
25 grams butter

1. Brown the lamb evenly in a dash of oil in a very hot, lidded frying pan.
2. Add the onion, pepper, dried fruit, tomatoes and water or beef stock and stir to mix.
3. Cover and simmer very gently for 35–40 minutes. Stand while preparing the couscous before serving.
4. Pour the boiling water or stock over the couscous, cover and stand for 10 minutes or until all the liquid has been absorbed. Add the butter, cover and microwave on high power for 5 minutes. Fluff with a fork and season with salt.

Serves 4

Moroccan lamb pilaf

In 2005, Food in a Minute was joined by co-sponsor SunRice which allowed us to present creative ways with rice, such as this pilaf. Add a few chopped pistachio nuts and dried apricots for extra colour, flavour and texture.

600 grams lean diced lamb
1 onion, peeled and sliced
1 tsp minced garlic
2 tsp minced ginger
400 gram can Wattie's Moroccan Style Tomatoes
½ cup chicken stock
1–2 tblsp chopped fresh coriander or parsley

Fragrant Rice

1 onion, peeled and finely sliced
1½ cups SunRice Basmati Indian Aromatic Rice
2¼ cups hot chicken stock
½ tsp turmeric
2–3 tblsp raisins
2 tblsp toasted slivered almonds

1. Brown the lamb in a dash of oil in a hot frying pan. This is best done in two batches. Set aside.

2. Add the onion, garlic and ginger and pan-fry until tender, but not brown. Stir in tomatoes, chicken stock and lamb to the sauce, cover and simmer gently 15–20 minutes. Stir in the coriander just before serving. Season if wished.

Fragrant Rice

3. Heat a dash of oil in a large lidded saucepan and cook the onion until just starting to colour. Add rice and stir for 1 minute. Stir in the hot chicken stock, with turmeric and raisins.

4. Cover and simmer for about 10 minutes. Remove from the heat and stand 5 minutes without lifting the lid. Scatter with toasted almonds.

Serves 4–5

Tuscan lamb shanks

Add more flavour to this easy casserole with additional Mediterranean ingredients: chopped capers, rosemary, pancetta or even a few anchovies.

4 lamb shanks
250 grams whole baby mushrooms, halved if large
1–2 onions, peeled and diced
420 gram can Wattie's Garlic Pasta Sauce
½ cup red wine or beef stock
2 cups black olives (optional)

1. Brown the lamb shanks evenly in a dash of oil in a hot frying pan. Transfer them to a casserole dish.

2. Scatter over the mushrooms and onion. Pour over the pasta sauce, red wine or beef stock and add the olives, if using.

3. Bake at 160°C for 1¼–1½ hours or until the lamb shanks are tender. Serve hot over mashed potato, polenta or pasta.

Serves 4

Boston baked beans

Boston baked beans is a classic American dish made with dried haricot beans which require overnight soaking and cooking. Using Wattie's Baked Beans means you can quickly prepare this nutritious low-fat dish, just the thing for a lazy winter weekend meal.

4 pork slices, rind removed
2 onions, peeled and finely chopped
1 tsp minced garlic
1 tblsp dry mustard
2 tblsp brown sugar
¼ cup golden syrup
2 x 420 gram cans Wattie's Baked Beans
¼ cup Lea & Perrins Worcestershire Sauce
¼ cup Wattie's Homestyle Tomato Sauce

1. Cut the pork into 1 cm wide pieces. Heat a dash of oil in a large, heat-proof casserole and cook the pork over a moderate heat until well browned.

2. Add the onion and garlic and cook for a further 2 minutes.

3. Add the mustard, brown sugar, golden syrup, baked beans, Worcestershire sauce and tomato sauce.

4. Stir, cover and simmer gently for about 10 minutes. Serve hot with toast for brunch or with green vegetables for dinner.

Serves 4

Golden plum pork loin chops

This is a fabulously easy way to cook pork chops.

12–16 prunes
2 tblsp port or red wine
6–8 lean boneless loin pork chops
½ cup Wattie's Bit on the Side Oriental Plum Sauce

2 spring onions
½ cup toasted cashews (preferably unsalted)

¼ cup Wattie's Bit on the Side Oriental Plum Sauce
¼ cup sour cream

1. Soak the prunes in the port or red wine for about 30 minutes.
2. Arrange the pork chops and prunes in a 6-cup capacity lasagne-style baking dish.
3. Spread over the oriental plum sauce.
4. Bake at 200°C for 25 minutes.
5. Finely chop the spring onions and cashews and sprinkle over the pork just before serving with the sauce.
7. For the sauce, blend the oriental plum sauce and sour cream together.

Serves 4–6

Macaroni cheese bake

During 2002 Wattie's launched canned Pasta Bake and Potato Bake sauces making family favourites such as macaroni cheese all that much easier for busy families.

2 cups Wattie's Frozen Mixed Vegetables
3 cups cooked pasta shapes
250 grams ham or 2 ham steaks, diced
2–3 spring onions, trimmed and sliced
6 sundried tomato halves, chopped (optional)
1 tblsp freshly chopped oregano or parsley
400 gram can Wattie's Macaroni Cheese Creamy Pasta Bake Sauce
¼ cup grated cheddar or parmesan cheese

1. Place the frozen vegetables into a microwave-proof bowl. Cover and microwave on high for 4 minutes or until defrosted and just warm.

2. Add the pasta, ham, spring onions, sundried tomatoes, oregano or parsley and the pasta sauce. Mix well and season with pepper if wished.

3. Turn into a shallow ovenproof dish and sprinkle with grated cheese.

4. Bake at 180°C for 35 minutes or until golden and hot.

Serves 4–5

Spanish pork chops with Mediterranean vegetable roasters

Liven up your family's dinnertime with this dish. Zesty chopped tomatoes and olives are married with pork chops, dried apricots and Wattie's Mediterranean Vegetable Roasters to produce a real crowd-pleaser.

4 x 100% New Zealand Pork Loin Chops
1 onion, peeled and chopped
400 gram can Wattie's Chopped Tomatoes with Olives
¼ cup finely sliced dried apricots
½ cup chicken stock
600 gram bag Wattie's Mediterranean Vegetable Roasters
1 tbsp chopped fresh parsley
1–2 tbsp chopped stuffed olives

1. Heat a frying pan with a dash of oil and lightly brown the pork loin chops on both sides quickly.
2. Add the onion to the pan and cook until tender. Add the chopped tomatoes, apricots and chicken stock, stir to combine.
3. Spoon half the tomato sauce into the base of an ovenproof dish. Arrange the browned pork chops on top, slightly overlapping each other. Spoon over the remaining sauce.
4. Scatter the vegetable roasters on a separate baking tray.
5. Bake both at 190°C for about 20 minutes or until the pork is golden and tender. Remove the pork, increase oven temperature to 220°C and continue to cook the roasters for a further 5 minutes or until crisp.
6. Serve the pork garnished with chopped parsley and chopped olives if wished and accompanied with the vegetable roasters.

Serves 4

Sweet apple and pork braise

Pork and fruit are natural partners and here we use Bit on the Side Absolutely Apple Sauce as a base for a family casserole. Don't forget the sage, it aids digestion.

- 500 grams New Zealand Trim Pork Leg Steaks
- 2 small onions, peeled and diced
- 2–3 stalks celery, trimmed and finely chopped
- 1 tsp minced fresh garlic
- ½ cup raisins or sultanas
- 1 tblsp chopped fresh sage or 1 tsp dried
- ½–1 300 gram bottle Wattie's Bit on the Side Absolutely Apple Sauce
- ½ cup chicken stock or water

1. Cut the pork into 3 cm pieces. Heat a dash of oil in a lidded frying pan and when very hot quickly brown the pork pieces on all sides.
2. Add the onions, celery, garlic, raisins or sultanas, sage, apple sauce and stock or water. Season with pepper and stir. (If only using half a bottle of apple sauce, add an extra half cup of stock or water.)
3. Cover and simmer on top of the stove over a low heat for 30 minutes or until the pork is tender.
4. Serve over mashed kumara or potato garnished with extra sage leaves.

Serves 4

Autumn sausages

Sausages are a winter favourite on Food in a Minute and this idea appeared in our first year on television.

6–8 thick beef sausages
1 large or 2 small swedes, peeled and diced
1 onion, peeled and diced
1 large or 2 small carrots, peeled and diced
3–4 stalks celery, diced, reserving the leaves
550 gram can Wattie's Just Add Hearty Savoury Mince Simmer Sauce
1 cup water

1. Brown the sausages in a frying pan until they are almost cooked. Remove, allow to cool slightly, then cut into thick rounds.

2. Add the swedes, onion, carrots and celery to the pan and toss quickly for 3–5 minutes to brown lightly.

3. Return sausages to the pan with the simmer sauce and water. Cover and simmer very gently for 30 minutes.

4. Finely slice the celery leaves, add to the sausages and season with pepper before serving with rice, pasta or potatoes.

Serves 4

Fruity devilled sausages

A super family dish for cooler nights. Add extra vegetables, such as sliced leek, carrots or parsnip, to make a one-pot meal.

8 really tasty, thick beef or pork sausages
1 apple, cored and sliced
1 onion, peeled and sliced
½ cup sultanas
227 gram can pineapple pieces and juice
560 gram can Wattie's Just Add Devilled Sausages Simmer Sauce

1. Heat 1 tblsp oil in a frying pan and add the sausages. Brown on both sides over a low heat so they do not split their skins.
2. Add the apple, onion, sultanas, pineapple and juice and can of simmer sauce.
3. Stir, cover and simmer over a low heat for 30 minutes.
4. Serve the sausages with plenty of hearty mashed potato and vegetables.

Serves 4

Sausage hot pot

Jazz up sausage meat with this recipe. Serve over rice with plenty of vegetables for a healthy meal. Try making this with a combination of sausage meat and minced pork.

500 grams sausage meat
¼ cup chopped parsley
¼ cup Wattie's Tomato Sauce
1 apple, peeled and grated
1 egg
dash of oil
545 gram can Wattie's Just Add Country French Mince Simmer Sauce
1 tsp cracked black pepper

1. In a bowl mix together the sausage meat, parsley, tomato sauce, apple, egg and season with pepper.
2. Using wet hands, roll the mixture into 20 even-shaped balls.
3. Heat the oil in a lidded frying pan and brown the sausage balls evenly on all sides.
4. Add the simmer sauce and black pepper. Stir, cover and simmer for 30 minutes over a low heat.
5. Serve with your favourite vegetables.

Serves 4

Winter sausages

An easy sausage casserole is quickly jazzed up with a savoury crumble in place of a mashed potato or pie topping.

6 thick, tasty sausages
2 stalks celery, trimmed and chopped
2 carrots, peeled and chopped
1 swede, peeled and chopped (or use parsnip)
550 gram can Wattie's Just Add Devilled Sausages Simmer Sauce
½ cup water

2 cups fresh breadcrumbs (white or wholemeal)
½ cup chopped parsley
½ cup grated cheddar cheese
75 grams butter, melted
salt and pepper

1. Cook the sausages in a lightly oiled, lidded frying pan until almost cooked. Set the sausages aside.
2. Add the celery, carrots and swede to the pan and toss quickly to brown.
3. Stir in the simmer sauce and water and cover. Simmer for 10 minutes or until the vegetables are almost cooked.
4. Slice the sausages into 2 cm rounds and place in a 6-cup capacity casserole. Pour over the vegetables and sauce.
5. To make the topping, put the breadcrumbs, parsley and cheese into a bowl and stir through the melted butter. Season with salt and pepper.
6. Sprinkle on top of the sausage mixture and bake at 180°C for 20–30 minutes until the topping is golden and the sausages cooked.

Serves 4

Spinach and feta filo pie

For filo to be deliciously crispy, cook it well otherwise it will be soggy underneath the top layer. Filo can be brushed with olive oil in place of butter, if you wish.

1 tblsp oil
2 onions, peeled and finely sliced
2 x 250 gram boxes Wattie's Frozen Chopped Spinach, defrosted
2 x 250 gram pottles Tararua Cottage Cheese
200 grams feta cheese, crumbled
3 tblsp chopped fresh oregano, marjoram, mint or parsley
4 tblsp butter, melted
16 sheets filo pastry
1–2 tblsp sesame seeds (optional)

1. Heat the oil in a frying pan and cook the onions for 3–5 minutes until tender. Cool.

2. Squeeze the spinach very firmly between two plates to drain off excess water. Mix together the spinach, cottage cheese, feta cheese, onion and herbs. Season with salt and pepper.

3. Butter 8 filo sheets and line a 2 cm deep pie dish. Spoon the spinach filling in evenly. Fold over the filo edges. Brush the remaining filo sheets with butter and arrange on top. Sprinkle with sesame seeds if wished.

4. Bake at 190°C (fan bake 170°C) for 35–40 minutes.

Serves 6

Flamenco pie

In this vegetable-laden pie, freezer favourites hash browns are used to make an easy no-fuss base.

2 tblsp oil
1 onion, peeled and finely chopped
500 grams lean minced beef
400 gram can Wattie's Mexican Style Tomatoes
¼ cup chopped stuffed olives (optional)
1 red pepper, finely chopped
¼ cup water
500 gram box Wattie's Hash Browns
1 carrot, peeled and grated
1 courgette, trimmed and grated
1 cup grated Edam cheese

1. Heat the oil in a frying pan and brown the onion and beef over a high heat.

2. Add the tomatoes, olives, red pepper and water. Stir well, cover and simmer for 20 minutes.

3. Heat a deep 26–28 cm ovenproof frying pan. Add the hash browns in one layer, cutting to fit where necessary. Cook for 5–7 minutes until warmed through then press with a fork to flatten — making a thick layer in the bottom of the pan.

4. Pour over the spicy meat mixture. Arrange the grated carrot and courgette on top and cover with the grated cheese.

5. Fan grill in the centre-middle section of the oven for about 10 minutes at 180°C or until the cheese is golden and the meal hot.

6. Serve in wedges.

Note: If you do not have a fan grill option on your oven, bake at 180°C for 20 minutes and then grill for 5–10 minutes until golden.

Serves 4–6

French beef and mushroom cottage pie

My first challenge to use potato pom poms was also Food in a Minute's greatest ever success. Using them to top a family cottage pie, in place of having to cook and mash potatoes, seemed to register with our viewers and we sold three months' worth of stock in under one week and ran out of product. It still remains a favourite and this is the original recipe.

1 onion, finely chopped
500 grams minced beef
135 gram can Wattie's Tomato Paste
545 gram can Wattie's Just Add Country French Mince Simmer Sauce
2 cups chopped mushrooms
about 1 cup Wattie's Frozen Peas and Corn
1 cup or half a can of water
500 gram bag Wattie's Potato Pom Poms
½ cup grated tasty cheddar cheese

1. Heat a dash of oil in a frying pan and brown the onion and minced beef, breaking up the beef with a fork as you go to ensure even-sized pieces.

2. Add the tomato paste and cook, stirring over a moderate heat until it has darkened in colour to a deeper brown shade. This takes about 5 minutes and adds a wonderful rich flavour to the pie.

3. Add the simmer sauce, mushrooms, peas and corn and water.

4. Stir, cover and simmer for 15 minutes. Stir occasionally.

5. Transfer to a 6-cup capacity ovenproof dish, top with pom poms and sprinkle over the grated cheddar cheese.

6. Bake at 220°C for about 15–20 minutes until the topping is golden, the cheese bubbling and the pie hot and delicious.

Serves 4–5

Chicken and spinach pies

These pies can be prepared earlier in the day (up to Step 6) and refrigerated until required. Bake straight from the fridge and allow an extra five minutes' cooking time.

4 boneless Tegel Chicken Breasts, skin removed
250 gram box Wattie's Frozen Chopped Spinach, defrosted
4 tblsp cream cheese
¼ tsp each nutmeg, salt and white pepper
2 sheets frozen pre-rolled puff pastry, defrosted
milk to glaze

1. Remove the skin from the chicken breasts.
2. Squeeze the spinach between two plates to remove all the excess moisture. (The spinach needs to be really dry to ensure that you do not end up with soggy pastry when the pies cook.)
3. Mix the spinach with the cream cheese, nutmeg, salt and pepper.
4. Take the pastry sheets and cut in half diagonally. Place a quarter of the spinach mixture in the centre of each triangle and place the chicken breast on top.
5. Bring the long ends down to cover the chicken and fold the thicker corner on top to completely enclose. Pinch ends together.
6. Transfer to a greased baking tray. Brush with milk to glaze.
7. Bake at 220 °C for 15–20 minutes until hot and golden.

Serves 4

Cranberry and chicken pie

This recipe can be made with a pre-cooked chicken or a smoked chicken. Just shred and add to the cooked onion.

1 double chicken breast, without skin
1 cup water
2 tblsp oil
1 onion, peeled and diced
2 tsp minced garlic
1–2 ham steaks, diced
½ cup Wattie's Bit on the Side Cracker Cranberry Sauce
2 tblsp sour cream
3 sheets pre-rolled puff pastry
milk to glaze

1. Put the chicken and water into a lidded frying pan and bring to a simmer. Poach for 20 minutes or until the chicken is cooked. Remove the chicken from the pan and cool.

2. Heat the oil in a frying pan and cook the onion and garlic until softened, not brown.

3. Shred the chicken and put in a bowl with the onion mixture, ham, cranberry sauce and sour cream.

4. Place 1 puff pastry sheet on a greased baking tray. Pile the chicken and ham filling on the top, leaving a 2 cm border around the outside. Brush the edge with milk.

5. Roll the remaining 2 sheets of pastry together, large enough to cover the top. Fold in half, leaving a 3 cm border around all edges. At right angles, cut 1 cm wide strips through the fold.

6. Open out and carefully place on top of the pie, pressing the edges together firmly. Trim the edges so they are even. Brush with milk to glaze.

7. Bake at 220°C for 30 minutes. Serve hot or cold in wedges.

Serves 6

Creamy chicken and corn pie

I enjoy pies in winter — all that delicious filling hidden under a fluffy golden baked pastry topping. Cool the filling if you can before topping with the pastry as steam from a warm filling (of any kind) will cause the pastry to be soggy underneath.

600 grams Tegel Boneless Chicken Thigh Fillets
1 leek, trimmed, washed and sliced
2–3 cups Wattie's Frozen Chuckwagon Corn
420 gram can Wattie's Condensed Creamy Chicken Soup
2 tblsp chopped fresh parsley
2 tblsp Tararua Sour Cream
2½ sheets pre-rolled puff pastry
milk or beaten egg to glaze

1. Cut chicken thighs into 3 pieces. Heat a dash of oil in a heavy-based frying pan and brown chicken evenly. Set aside.
2. Pan-fry the leek gently in remaining oil until softened. Add frozen corn, stirring for 2–3 minutes until thawed. Remove from heat and add soup, parsley, sour cream and reserved chicken. Season with pepper. Cool.
3. Roll the 2 sheets of pastry out together, large enough to cover the top of a 24 cm pie dish. Cut the remaining half pastry sheet into 2–3 cm strips.
4. Wet the edge of the pie dish and place the strips of pastry around the edge. Spoon in the filling. Brush the pastry edge with water, carefully roll the pastry lid over the filling and press the edges together firmly. Trim the pastry, so the edges are even. Brush with milk or beaten egg glaze.
5. Bake at 220°C for 30 minutes or until the pastry is well risen and golden.

Serves 4–6

Creamy smoked chicken filo pie

In the early days of Food in a Minute we didn't often use filo pastry (back in 1996 we were still getting used to handling it) but this recipe was a huge hit. Filo is easy to work with and with the scrunched-up uneven but decorative topping, it didn't matter how the finished pie was put together — once cooked, it looked and tasted fabulous.

2 small–medium red onions, peeled and sliced
250 grams sliced button mushrooms
2 tblsp chopped marjoram or oregano
2 tblsp sliced sundried tomato (optional)
1 Tegel Smoked Chicken
250 gram pottle Tararua Crème Fraîche
12 sheets filo pastry
100 grams butter, melted

1. Cook the onions in a dash of oil in a hot pan for 3 minutes. Add mushrooms and cook for a further 5 minutes or until they begin to soften. Add herbs and sundried tomatoes (if using) and cool.

2. Tear the smoked chicken into bite-sized pieces (discarding skin and bones). Toss into the mushroom mixture with the crème fraîche and season with salt and pepper.

3. Brush 8 sheets of filo pastry with the melted butter and place in a 24 cm flan tin. Fill with the chicken and mushroom mixture and then flip the overhanging filo pastry edges into the centre. Brush the remaining sheets of filo with butter and place on top of the pie. Sprinkle with sesame seeds if wished and bake at 190°C for 40–45 minutes until golden and crispy.

Serves 6

Pumpkin and chicken pie

A variation of our classic Food in a Minute cottage pie. Try one of these additional twists: add ham in place of bacon and mix in a teaspoon or two of dried tarragon, or use sherry in place of wine and cream in place of sour cream.

500 grams Tegel Boneless Chicken Meat
1 leek, washed and trimmed
3–4 rashers bacon, diced,
420 gram can Wattie's Condensed Creamy Pumpkin Soup
½ cup sour cream
½ cup chicken stock or water or white wine
1 tblsp freshly chopped parsley
500 gram bag Wattie's Potato Pom Poms
½ cup grated cheese

1. Cut chicken meat into 3–4 cm pieces. Heat a dash of oil in a heavy-based frying pan and brown chicken pieces evenly. Remove from the pan and keep warm.

2. Cut leek into 1 cm slices, fry in residue oil with bacon until softened and fragrant.

3. Remove from the heat and stir in soup, sour cream, chicken stock and parsley, season with salt and pepper.

4. Place cooked chicken in an ovenproof serving dish and pour over pumpkin sauce. Top with potato pom poms and sprinkle with grated cheese.

5. Bake at 190°C for 30 minutes or until piping hot and the pom poms are golden.

Serves 4–6

Winter chicken pie

Here we wanted to create a quick and easy recipe that required very little preparation. We thought that many people have leftover roast chicken either from one they cook or a bought ready-roasted chicken and so this would show how easily you can create a tasty meal from leftovers.

25 grams butter
2 leeks, well washed and finely sliced
2 tsp minced garlic
½ cooked chicken, shredded
420 gram can Wattie's Condensed Creamy Chicken Soup
½ cup sour cream
1 cup water or chicken stock
2–3 tblsp chopped parsley
500 gram bag Wattie's Potato Pom Poms

1. Melt the butter in a saucepan and cook the leeks until just tender. Add the garlic and cook for a further minute.

2. Remove from the heat and stir in the chicken, soup, sour cream, water or chicken stock and parsley.

3. Place the mixture into an 8-cup capacity ovenproof dish. Top with the potato pom poms.

4. Bake at 180°C for 40 minutes or until piping hot.

Serves 4–5

Smoked fish pie with garlic bread crust

One-pot meals are Food in a Minute flagship recipes. Here an easy crunchy topping is prepared from a simple loaf of French bread.

750 gram bag Wattie's Frozen Winter Veges Recipe Mix
250–400 grams smoked fish, flaked
400 gram can Wattie's Macaroni Cheese Pasta Bake Sauce
½ cup light cream, light sour cream or light crème fraîche
2 tblsp wholeseed mustard (or 1 tblsp wholeseed and 1 tblsp prepared mustard)
½ loaf French bread, sliced
garlic butter for spreading

1. Place the winter vegetables into a large bowl, cover and microwave on high power (100%) for 5–6 minutes, or until defrosted.

2. Add the flaked smoked fish, the cheese sauce, light cream and mustard and stir well. Transfer to a lasagne-style dish.

3. Spread the French bread slices with the garlic butter and layer on top of the smoked fish mixture.

4. Bake at 180°C for 30 minutes or until hot and golden.

Serves 4–5

Thai-scented burgers, page 124

Roasts & grills

Asian beef kebabs 120

Glazed meatloaf 122

Thai-scented burgers 124

Coconut chicken 125

Herb roast chicken with sage and onion roasters 126

Sweet chilli chicken with pawpaw salsa 127

Cranberry turkey 128

Roast turkey with oriental plum stuffing and sauce 129

Thai-scented roast Christmas turkey 130

Barbecued apricot-glazed ham with mustard fruits 131

New Zealand ham with orange, sweet chilli and rum glaze 132

Lea & Perrins ginger lamb chops 133

Quick winter roast lamb 134

Barbecued pork loin with sage and onion roasters 136

Barbecued sticky glazed ribs 137

Roast pork with sage and apple sauce 138

Asian beef kebabs

Cut the beef into large pieces to make juicy kebabs and add chopped vegetables to the skewers if you wish, such as sliced red onion, red peppers or mushrooms.

500–750 grams rump steak or scotch fillet steak
1 tsp minced garlic
1 tsp minced ginger
1 tsp minced chilli
2 tblsp sweet soy sauce (kecap manis)
2 tblsp oyster sauce

Peanut dip

½ cup Eta Peanut Butter
2 tblsp sweet soy sauce (kecap manis)
½ cup hot water

Yoghurt chilli dipping sauce

¼ cup non-fat plain yoghurt
¼ cup chilli sauce
2 tblsp chopped fresh mint

1. Cut the beef steak into large 3 cm cubes and place in a snaplock bag with the garlic, ginger, chilli and soy and oyster sauces. Seal the bag and toss to coat evenly. Refrigerate for 1 hour or up to 1 day.

2. Thread onto 6 bamboo skewers and barbecue over a moderately high heat for about 6–8 minutes until the meat is well browned but still moist.

3. To make the peanut dip mix all the ingredients together. To make the yoghurt chilli dipping sauce mix all the ingredients together.

4. Serve kebabs with salad accompanied with one or both sauces.

Serves 4–6

Glazed meatloaf

Meatloaves are super family foods and this basic recipe can easily be altered by adding a handful or two of dried fruit such as currants, raisins or chopped prunes. You can also vary the flavour by using any one of the Wattie's tomato sauce range.

½ cup cooked barley or rice (brown rice is great)
500 grams New Zealand Quality Mark Minced Beef
2 tblsp chopped fresh oregano, or use 1 tsp dried
2 tblsp chopped fresh parsley
2 tblsp chopped fresh thyme, or use 1 tsp dried
¼ cup Wattie's Tomato Sauce
2 spring onions, finely chopped
2 tsp minced garlic
1 egg

Glaze
2 tblsp honey
2 tblsp oil
2 tblsp Wattie's Tomato Sauce
2 tblsp soy sauce

1. In a bowl mix together the cooked barley or rice, mince, oregano, parsley, thyme, tomato sauce, spring onions, garlic and egg. Season well with salt and pepper.

2. Shape into a loaf and set in an ovenproof dish, such as a lasagne dish.

3. To make the glaze, mix the honey, oil, tomato sauce and soy sauce together and brush the glaze over the top.

4. Bake at 180°C for 60 minutes.

5. Stand for 10 minutes before carving.

6. Serve with your favourite vegetables and sauce to accompany.

Serves 6

Thai-scented burgers

Full of delicious Thai flavours such as mint, lemon grass, garlic, ginger and chilli, these burgers appeared around the summer of 1998 when Wattie's Bit on the Side range was new to the market.

- 500 grams Quality Mark Lean Minced Beef
- 2 tblsp chopped lemon grass
- 1 tblsp grated fresh ginger
- 3 cloves garlic, crushed, peeled and chopped
- 2 tsp ground coriander
- 1 tsp each salt and pepper
- 2 tblsp chopped fresh mint
- 2 tblsp chopped fresh coriander
- 2 spring onions, trimmed and chopped
- 1 cup fresh breadcrumbs
- 1 egg
- ½ cup Wattie's Bit on the Side Sweet Chilli Sauce

1. In a bowl put the mince, lemon grass, ginger, garlic, ground coriander, salt and pepper, fresh mint and coriander, spring onions, breadcrumbs, egg and chilli sauce and mix well. If you can, allow the mixture to stand for about 30 minutes.

2. Mould into 6 even-shaped burgers.

3. Barbecue or pan-fry the burgers over a moderate heat for 5–7 minutes each side, turning only once. Alternatively, grill the burgers.

4. Serve the burgers on a grilled or toasted bun, with a slice of grilled pineapple and crispy lettuce.

Serves 6

Coconut chicken

Delicious in summer. Cook the chicken over a moderate heat to prevent the honey in the marinade from burning and, if you're in a hurry, use Wattie's Condensed Pumpkin Soup in place of the pumpkin puree.

4 Tegel Single Chicken Breasts or 8–10 Boneless Chicken Thigh Portions
grated rind and juice from 2 lemons or 4 limes
1 tblsp chopped fresh coriander or parsley
1 tblsp grated fresh ginger
¼ cup coconut milk
1 tblsp honey
425 gram can Wattie's Stir Fry Creamy Satay Sauce
½ cup coconut milk
1 cup cooked pumpkin puree or Wattie's Condensed Pumpkin Soup
2 tblsp chopped cashew nuts

1. Cut 3 deep cuts in the skin of each chicken breast or thigh portion.

2. Mix together the lemon or lime rind and juice, coriander or parsley, ginger, coconut milk and honey and pour over the chicken. Turn to coat. Cover and marinate in the refrigerator for 30 minutes. Brush off excess marinade.

3. BBQ over a moderately hot heat or cook in a hot lightly oiled frying pan for 15–18 minutes by placing skin side down first and then turning half-way through the cooking time. Alternatively grill.

4. Mix the satay sauce with the coconut milk, pumpkin puree and cashews and simmer gently for 5 minutes.

5. Serve the chicken on grilled pineapple with the satay sauce and plenty of summer salads.

Serves 4

Herb roast chicken with sage and onion roasters

When roasting a whole chicken at home, I am more than likely to split it and flatten the bird, as in this recipe. It is quicker and, by cooking the chicken in a pan, I can use all the juices to make a quick sauce to accompany it.

1 fresh Tegel Tender Basted Chicken
50 grams butter
2 tblsp flour
2 rashers bacon, chopped
1 tblsp each chopped rosemary, thyme, sage and freshly ground black pepper
1 cup dry white wine
1 cup chicken stock
700 gram bag Wattie's Sage and Onion Roasters

1. Split the chicken down the backbone and flatten the bird.
2. Heat half of the butter in an ovenproof frying pan and place the chicken in and allow it to cook over a moderate heat for 2–3 minutes.
3. Sift the flour on top. Dot the remaining butter over, scatter over the bacon and herbs and season well with pepper.
4. Bake at 190°C for 45 minutes. Remove the chicken from the pan and set aside. Add the wine and boil to reduce by half. Stir in the stock to the pan and simmer for 1–2 minutes, before seasoning with black pepper. Serve the sauce with the chicken, potatoes and seasonal vegetables.
5. Scatter the roasters on a baking tray and add to the chicken in the last 30 minutes of cooking time.
6. When you remove the chicken from the oven, increase the heat to 230°C for 5 minutes to crisp the roasters while you make the chicken sauce.

Serves 6

Sweet chilli chicken with pawpaw salsa

This recipe, presented in 1997, showcased a new range of products called 'Bit on the Side'. The name caused outrage in 1997–1998 — a number of consumers thought it was highly offensive. At the time it was controversial, but today Bit on the Side sauces have become household staples and, as this recipe shows, can easily add spice and flavour to a simple baked chicken.

1 whole Tegel Chicken
¼ cup Wattie's Bit on the Side Sweet Chilli Sauce

½ pawpaw
2 spring onions, trimmed and finely chopped
2 tblsp Wattie's Bit on the Side Sweet Chilli Sauce
1 tsp finely minced fresh ginger (optional)

1. Rinse the chicken out well, removing any giblets. Pat dry.
2. Using kitchen scissors, cut down either side of the backbone of the chicken and discard.
3. Place the chicken breast side up on a chopping board and press down gently to flatten. Tuck the wings underneath. Using a sharp knife, cut about 6 deep slashes in the chicken right through the meat.
4. Spread the chicken with half the sweet chilli sauce and rub into the skin.
5. Bake in the centre of a 190°C oven for 1 hour. Spread the remaining sweet chilli sauce on top and bake a further 30–40 minutes until the chicken is golden brown. If the chicken begins to brown too much, cover the top with foil until the chicken is cooked.

7. To make the salsa scoop the seeds from the pawpaw. Peel then cut the fruit into 1 cm dice. Mix gently with spring onions, sweet chilli sauce and fresh ginger, if used. This salsa is nicer if it has been allowed to stand for at least 1 hour before serving. Serve with the chicken and summer vegetables.

Serves 6

Cranberry turkey

Serving cranberry sauce or jelly with turkey has become very vogue in the last few years and, to meet the demand, Wattie's launched the Cracker Cranberry Sauce. It's super in this dressing or mixed with a little vodka to serve on the side.

4.5 kg defrosted frozen Tegel Turkey
1 peeled and diced onion
2 tsp minced fresh garlic
4 rashers bacon, diced
2 cups fresh white breadcrumbs or cooked rice
grated rind of two oranges
½ cup raisins or dried cranberries
300 gram bottle Wattie's Bit on the Side Cracker Cranberry Sauce
50 grams softened butter
2 tblsp honey

1. Wash the turkey and pat dry using paper towels.
2. Heat a dash of oil in a frying pan and cook the onion, garlic and bacon until softened.
3. Add the breadcrumbs, orange rind, raisins, ½ cup cranberry sauce and mix together. Season well with salt and pepper.
4. Fill the turkey cavity with the stuffing. Tie the turkey legs together and twist the wings under the body.
5. Spread the butter on top of the turkey and place into a roasting dish. Cook according to the times on the back of the turkey pack.
6. Mix the remaining cranberry sauce with the honey and during the last 20 minutes of cooking time, brush the turkey regularly to glaze.

Serves 8–10

Roast turkey with oriental plum stuffing and sauce

Each Christmas we have a brainstorming session to think up new ideas for the traditional festive fare and this recipe appeared around 2003. The sauce is particularly delicious with the plums and port combined with the pan juices. This stuffing would also be nice in a roast chicken, just halve the quantities.

4 kg Tegel Frozen Tender Basted Turkey size 4
1 onion, peeled and chopped
1 tblsp minced ginger
300 grams fresh plums, halved, stoned and diced
3 cups fresh white breadcrumbs
¼ cup freshly chopped parsley
1 egg, beaten
300 gram bottle Wattie's Bit on the Side Oriental Plum Sauce
grated rind of one orange
½ cup fresh orange juice
¼ cup port
½ cup chicken stock

1. Defrost the turkey according to the instructions on the packet. Rinse the packet, then take note of the cooking instructions.

2. Gently cook the onion and ginger in a dash of oil, until tender, but not brown.

3. In a bowl mix together the onion and ginger, plums, breadcrumbs, parsley, egg, ½ cup plum sauce and season with salt and pepper. Use to fill the cavity of the turkey. Tie the legs together and twist the wings underneath.

4. Roast according to the directions on the back of the turkey packet. Remove from the oven, cover and rest for 15 minutes before carving.

5. Drain cooking juices from roasting pan, discarding any fat. In a small saucepan stir together the cooking juices, orange rind and juice, port, stock and remaining plum sauce until warm.

6. Serve the turkey with your favourite roasted vegetables and the hot plum sauce.

Serves 8

Thai-scented roast Christmas turkey

Deliciously non-traditional and can be enjoyed at any time of the year.

850 grams Tegel Boneless Turkey Roast
6 peeled baby orange-fleshed kumara
3 parsnips, peeled and halved
3 carrots, peeled and halved
8–10 kaffir lime leaves (optional)
2 red peppers, cut into thirds and deseeded
3 courgettes, trimmed and halved
½ bottle Wattie's Bit on the Side Sweet Chilli Sauce
¼ cup oil

1. Defrost the turkey roast in the refrigerator as directed on the packet.

2. Place the turkey roast on a baking paper-lined tray and place in a 180°C oven for 30 minutes.

3. Toss the kumara, parsnips and carrots with half the chilli sauce and the oil. Scatter the kaffir lime leaves around the turkey and then arrange the vegetables on top. Return to the oven for a further 30 minutes.

4. Toss the red peppers and courgettes with the remaining chilli sauce and oil and scatter around the vegetables. Return to the oven for a further 30–40 minutes until the turkey is cooked and the vegetables lovely and crispy. Glaze the turkey with the chilli sauce when removed from the oven.

Serves 5–6

Barbecued apricot-glazed ham with mustard fruits

This recipe was created by my food assistant Ann Boardman for Christmas 2005. The fruits are particularly delicious and work well with the fruit-glazed ham. If you do not have mustard seeds, use a grainy mustard instead.

- 100% New Zealand Pork Cooked Half Ham on the Bone
- about 2 tblsp whole cloves
- 300 gram bottle Wattie's Bit on the Side Spiced Apricot Sauce
- 500 gram selection of dried fruits (apricots, figs, prunes, apples)
- 3 firm ripe pears, peeled, cored and quartered
- ½ tropical gold pineapple, skinned and sliced into wedges
- 565 gram can lychees in syrup
- 2 tblsp yellow mustard seeds
- ½ cup brown sugar
- ¾ cup dry white wine
- ½ cup white wine vinegar
- 1½–2 tsp mustard powder

1. Carefully run your fingers under the skin of the ham and lift it away. Do this slowly so you finish with a smooth layer of fat that will glaze beautifully. Place on a rack in a foil-lined baking tray.

2. Using a small sharp knife, cut ham fat layer into a criss-cross diamond pattern. Decorate ham with whole cloves. Brush half a cup of apricot sauce over the ham. Pour 2 cups water around the ham.

3. In a separate smaller foil-lined baking tray, put the dried fruits, pears, pineapple, lychees and syrup, mustard seeds, brown sugar, wine, vinegar and mustard powder with 1 cup water. Stir gently to mix.

4. Pre-heat lidded barbecue to 200°C, place ham tray in the centre of the barbecue. Cover and return to temperature, this will take about 15 minutes. Turn the gas to low and cook at 200°C for 1¾ hours or until hot through the bone.

5. Add the tray of mustard fruits to the barbecue for the final 45 minutes' cooking time. Stir through remaining apricot sauce into the warm mustard fruits. Serve ham hot or cold, accompanied with the fruits.

Oven cooking method

- Bake in the oven at 180°C for 30–40 minutes, brushing with glaze every 10 minutes. To serve hot, bake at 160°C, allowing 20 minutes per kilogram, brushing with glaze every 10 minutes, until it has all been used.

New Zealand ham with orange, sweet chilli and rum glaze

One of my food team members, Tracey Sunderland, created this recipe back in about 2000 and I can still remember her saying 'you can't glaze a ham without alcohol'. Tracey spiked the chilli sauce with a good pouring of dark rum and, coupled with the oranges, this quickly became one of our best-ever glazes for flavour.

3½ kg cooked New Zealand ham on the bone*
2 oranges, finely sliced
about 12 whole cloves
300 gram bottle Wattie's Bit on the Side Sweet Chilli Sauce
½ cup rum or orange juice

1. Carefully lift the skin from the cooked ham by running clean fingers between the skin and ham. It will come away easily.
2. Arrange overlapping layers of orange slices over the ham, securing each orange slice with a whole clove and/or toothpicks.
3. Mix together the chilli sauce and rum or orange juice and brush the orange-covered ham liberally with half of this glazing mix.
4. Bake the ham at 180°C for 35–40 minutes. (To serve hot, bake the ham at 160°C for 20 minutes per 1 kg, brushing with the glaze every 10–15 minutes.)
5. Bring the remaining chilli and rum glaze to the boil before serving hot or cold with the ham.

Serves 8–10

*To store your ham, cover loosely with foil, a clean damp towel or ham bag and place in the refrigerator, changing the covering daily.

Lea & Perrins ginger lamb chops

When you remove the lamb chops from the marinade, pat them dry before cooking. If you do not have sherry at home, use red wine.

¼ cup Lea & Perrins Worcestershire Sauce
¼ cup sherry
1 tblsp minced ginger
4–6 lamb loin chops

1. Mix together the Worcestershire sauce, sherry and ginger and pour into a snaplock bag. Add the lamb loin chops, seal and toss to coat in the marinade. Refrigerate for up to 2 hours.

2. Pan-fry the lamb chops in a dash of oil in a hot frying pan, or grill under a high heat, turning once only.

Serves 4

Quick winter roast lamb

This simple roast appeared around 1997 and it's still an ideal recipe for a family today, as everything is cooked in one dish in the oven. No-fuss cooking at its best.

1 New Zealand Quality Mark loin lamb with about 10 chops
Lea & Perrins Worcestershire Sauce
1 tsp minced garlic
2 onions, peeled and sliced
2 parsnips, peeled and sliced
250–300 grams pumpkin, sliced
½ x 750 gram bag Wattie's Frozen Whole Baby Beans
½ cup Eta Lite and Free Garden Herb Dressing

1. Score the loin lamb on the skin side and season well with Worcestershire sauce. Turn over and season the meat well with more Worcestershire sauce and garlic. Roll up the flap and tie the loin securely with string or secure with skewers.

2. Toss the onions, parsnips and pumpkin in a little oil and place in a shallow roasting dish. Sit the lamb on top.

3. Fan bake at 200°C for 35 minutes (or bake at 220°C for 45 minutes).

4. Transfer the lamb to a plate and sprinkle the beans into the baking dish, toss and return to the oven for 5 minutes. Remove and toss the vegetables with the herb dressing.

5. Carve the lamb into chops and serve over the hot vegetable salad.

Serves 4

Barbecued pork loin with sage and onion roasters

This summer (2005/2006) we decided to roast pork on the barbecue, given the number of New Zealanders who have one. It was a great success. The simple stuffing, made from apples and sage, is both easy to prepare and partners pork well.

½ onion, peeled and finely chopped
1 stalk celery, trimmed and finely diced
380 gram can Wattie's Diced Apple
2 tblsp freshly chopped sage
3 cups fresh white breadcrumbs
1 egg, beaten
2 kg 100% New Zealand Pork Boneless Loin Roast, with a long flap, well scored
700 gram bag Wattie's Sage and Onion Roasters
1 red onion, peeled and cut into wedges
1 red and yellow pepper, deseeded and cut into 2 cm strips

1. Gently cook the onion and celery in a dash of oil until tender, but not brown. Mix together the apple, sage, breadcrumbs, egg and the cooked onion and celery. Season with salt and pepper. Cool.

2. Place the pork skin side down on a chopping board, arrange half the stuffing down the centre pork loin. Bring the flap over to enclose the stuffing and tie securely with string. Rub the skin well with oil and sprinkle with salt.

3. Pre-heat the barbecue to 230°C. Place prepared pork on a rack in a foil-lined roasting tin, placing a meat thermometer into the thickest part of the pork. Barbecue the pork in the centre of the barbecue, only use the burners either side of the pork, not under the pork. Cover and keep the temperature as close to 200°C as possible, allowing 30 minutes per 500 grams cooking time, or about 2 hours in total. Pork is cooked when it reaches an internal temperature of 71°C. Remove the cooked pork and allow the roast to rest 15 minutes before carving.

4. Roll the remaining stuffing into balls. Lightly oil barbecue plate and cook the sage and onion roasters over a moderate heat for 6–7 minutes each side with stuffing balls, red onion and peppers. Serve the pork loin sliced with roasted vegetables and stuffing balls.

Serves 10

Barbecued sticky glazed ribs

Delicious, sweet and savoury, just the way spare ribs are meant to be. HP sauce is another product Wattie's markets here in New Zealand and it takes its name from the Houses of Parliament. Originally made in Birmingham, the manufacturer changed the name in the early 1900s when he heard that a restaurant in the Houses of Parliament (London) was serving the sauce. Its malty flavour works well with the peaches and ginger.

1.5–1.8 kg 100% New Zealand Pork Spare Ribs
410 gram can Oak Peach Slices in Syrup
½ cup HP sauce
1 tblsp minced ginger
½ cup water

Spicy peach salsa
410 gram can Oak Peach Slices in Syrup, drained
½ red onion, peeled and finely chopped
1 tsp minced red chilli
1 tblsp freshly chopped mint
3 tblsp HP sauce
1 tblsp lemon or lime juice

1. Cut the pork into 2–3 rib pieces. Set aside.
2. Process the peaches in syrup, HP sauce, ginger and water in a food processor or blender until smooth.
3. Pour the peach marinade into a large saucepan with the ribs. Cover and bring to the boil, reduce heat and simmer gently for 30–35 minutes, stirring occasionally. Remove the ribs from the saucepan and set aside. Simmer the marinade until reduced by half.
4. Barbecue cooked ribs, over a medium heat, for 10–15 minutes, brushing with the peach marinade until sticky and golden.
5. To make the salsa, roughly chop the peaches and combine with red onion, chilli, mint, HP sauce and lemon or lime juice, mix well.
6. Serve the ribs and salsa with barbecued vegetables.

Serves 6

Roast pork with sage and apple sauce

Throughout our time on Food in a Minute we have encouraged New Zealanders to use a thermometer to cook their pork to ensure that it is not overcooked and remains juicy. A thermometer is a worthwhile addition to your kitchen, as it can be used for all roasts.

2.5–3 kg 100% NZ Pork Leg Roast
1 small bunch fresh sage
300 gram bottle Wattie's Bit on the Side Absolutely Apple Sauce
1 tblsp freshly chopped sage

1. Rub the pork leg liberally with oil and salt, arrange the washed sage on a rack in a baking tray, place the pork on top.

2. Fan bake at 220°C for 20 minutes, then lower the oven temperature to 160°C and cook, allowing 30 minutes per 500 grams of meat. To test if it's ready, pierce the pork with a skewer at the thickest part through to the bone; if the juices run clear, the pork is cooked. Alternatively, use a meat thermometer and cook the pork to 71°C. If the meat is not cooked, continue to cook for a further 15 minutes before testing again. Cover and rest the pork for 15 minutes before carving.

3. Drain cooking juices from the roasting pan. Combine in a small saucepan with apple sauce and freshly chopped sage, heat gently, do not boil.

4. Serve the roast pork slices with pieces of crackling, warm sage and apple sauce and your favourite roast vegetables.

Serves 8–10

Thai green pork curry, page 148

Curries

Weekday curry	142
Butter chicken	143
Fish in sweet curry sauce	144
Curried lamb pies with ginger kumara mash	145
Lamb curry with potatoes and spinach	146
Indian pork korma	147
Thai green pork curry	148
Autumn vegetables and bean korma curry	150
Lentil and vegetable butter curry	151
Curried winter vegetables	152

Weekday curry

Adding lentils or short grain rice to lean beef mince makes deliciously textured meatballs, with extra fibre. Originally this recipe called for Madras Curry Sauce, but as this is now deleted, I have altered this healthy recipe to use another Wattie's curry sauce.

½ cup red lentils
1 onion, peeled and finely diced
500 grams Quality Mark Lean Minced Beef
1 egg
1 tsp each ground coriander, cumin and garam masala, or use 1 tblsp curry powder
1 tsp salt
1 tsp black pepper
2 tblsp oil
405 gram can Wattie's Butter Chicken Curry Sauce
3 large tomatoes, finely chopped
¼ cup chopped fresh coriander or parsley
plain unsweetened yoghurt and fresh coriander leaves (to garnish)

1. Soak the lentils in 1 cup water for 30 minutes. Drain well.
2. In a bowl mix together the lentils, onion, mince, egg, coriander, cumin, garam masala or curry powder, salt and pepper. Shape into 12 even-sized meatballs.
3. Heat the oil in a lidded frying pan and brown the meatballs on all sides over a moderate heat.
4. Add the curry sauce and tomatoes and stir. Cover and simmer gently for 30 minutes until the meatballs are cooked. Stir in the chopped coriander or parsley.
5. Serve over boiled rice garnished with yoghurt and coriander.

Serves 4

Butter chicken

When Wattie's launched their Indian Style Tomatoes, we created this recipe. It remains one of my favourites and I often cook this recipe at home as the curry flavour is mild. For an extra creamy flavour, use mascarpone in place of cream.

6 Tegel Chicken Leg And Thigh Portions
1 medium onion, peeled and quartered
1 cup Naturalea Plain Unsweetened Yoghurt
1 tsp each ground ginger and garam masala
¼ tsp chilli powder
2 x 400 gram cans Wattie's Indian Style Tomatoes
½ cup cream
an oversized knob of butter (about 50 grams)
2 tblsp chopped coriander (optional)

1. Cut the chicken portions in half and then remove the skin. Slash each portion deeply in three places. Place in one layer in a non-metallic dish.

2. In a food processor, process the onion, yoghurt and spices. Pour over the chicken and turn to coat evenly. Cover and refrigerate for at least 1 hour or up to 8 hours. (The longer you can leave the chicken to marinate, the more intense the flavour will be.)

3. Remove the chicken from the marinade, brush off any excess. Bake on a grill tray at 230°C for 20–25 minutes until well browned and cooked.

4. While the chicken is cooking prepare the sauce. Simmer the two cans of Indian tomatoes in a saucepan until reduced by half. Stir in the cream, butter and coriander and keep warm. Do not boil, or the sauce will curdle.

5. Serve the chicken coated in the butter sauce. Serve with rice, poppadums, chutneys, fresh bananas — sliced, tossed in lemon juice and desiccated coconut.

Serves 4–6

Fish in sweet curry sauce

This dish requires a fish that will hold together while it is being cooked in the sauce. Use bluenose, groper, hapuka, snapper, blue cod, dory, tuna or gurnard.

2 x 400 gram cans Wattie's Indian Style Tomatoes
4 x 150 gram pieces medium to firm white fish fillets
1–1½ cups Wattie's Frozen Cross Cut Green Beans
2 tblsp chopped fresh coriander

Banana and ginger raita
1 banana, peeled and diced
1 cup non-fat unsweetened yoghurt
1 tsp minced fresh ginger
pinch of salt

1. Put the tomatoes into a lidded frying pan and simmer gently until they are reduced by one-third.
2. Arrange the fish fillets on top in one layer and cook for 3 minutes.
3. Turn the fish over and sprinkle the green beans on top.
4. Cover and simmer gently for 5–8 minutes until the fish is cooked. Sprinkle over the coriander. The cooking time will depend on the thickness of the fish fillets.
5. To make the banana and ginger raita, mix all the ingredients together. Serve the fish on rice with the raita and poppadums.

Serves 4

Curried lamb pies with ginger kumara mash

A spicy variation on a cottage pie. Originally the recipe called for Rogan Josh Curry Sauce, but this has since been deleted, so I have adapted this recipe to use Korma Curry Sauce instead.

500 grams Quality Mark Lean Leg Lamb Steaks
¼ cup Wattie's Tomato Paste
1 leek, trimmed, rinsed and finely chopped
1 carrot, peeled and finely chopped
410 gram can Wattie's Korma Curry Sauce

Ginger and kumara mash
750 grams kumara, peeled and chopped
butter and milk for mashing
1 tsp ground ginger

1. Cut the lamb steaks into 1 cm dice. Heat a dash of oil in a frying pan and brown the meat over a high heat. Add the tomato paste and cook for 2–3 minutes, stirring until the paste becomes much darker in colour.

2. Stir in the leek, carrot and curry sauce. Lower the heat, cover and simmer for 10 minutes.

3. Divide the curry between four individual serving dishes and pile the ginger and kumara mash on top.

4. Bake at 200°C for 10 minutes.

5. To make the ginger and kumara mash, cook the kumara in boiling salted water until tender. Drain and mash with a knob of butter and a good pouring of milk. Add the ground ginger, season with salt and pepper and beat until smooth.

Serves 4

Lamb curry with potatoes and spinach

An easy Indian meal — all you need is some poppadums and your favourite chutneys.

1 kg lean shoulder lamb
2 onions, peeled and finely sliced
2 tomatoes, chopped
2 tblsp Indian curry paste
400 gram can Wattie's Indian Style Tomatoes
yoghurt
chopped fresh coriander to garnish

1 onion, peeled and finely sliced
2 cloves garlic, peeled and chopped
2 large potatoes, peeled and cut into 4 cm pieces
250 gram bag Wattie's Frozen Free Flow Spinach, defrosted
½ tsp each curry powder and garam masala
½ cup water

1. Trim any excess fat from the lamb. Cut the meat into large pieces, about 3 cm.
2. Heat a dash of oil in a large lidded frying pan until hot. Add the lamb and brown quickly over a moderately high heat.
3. Add the onions, tomatoes, curry paste and canned tomatoes. Bring to the boil, cover and simmer for 15 minutes then remove the lid and simmer a further 15 minutes.
4. Allow to stand for 5 minutes before garnishing with yoghurt and chopped coriander. Serve with potatoes and spinach.

Potatoes and spinach

1. Cook the onion in a lidded frying pan in a dash of oil over a moderate to high heat for 2–3 minutes.
2. Add the garlic, potatoes, spinach, curry powder, garam masala and water and stir together.
3. Cover and simmer gently for 20 minutes or until the potatoes are just cooked. There should be very little moisture left. Season with salt and pepper to serve.

Serves 4–5

Indian pork korma

When we started Food in a Minute, only a few curry sauces were available. Over the years Wattie's has created a curry sauce range to meet demands for more international meals. Then, within the last few years, Wattie's has moved further to create more authentic curry sauces which are ideal to serve two or four.

500 grams 100% New Zealand Pork Stir Fry or Pork Schnitzel (cut into 1–2 cm strips)
1 onion, peeled and chopped
250 grams waxy red-skinned potatoes, washed and diced into 1.5 cm pieces
410 gram can Wattie's Korma Curry Sauce
400 gram can Wattie's Indian Style Tomatoes
½ cup Naturalea Plain Unsweetened Yoghurt
2 tblsp fresh chopped coriander

1. Quickly stir-fry the pork in a hot wok or frying pan in a dash of oil, until golden. Set aside.
2. Cook onion until just beginning to soften, add potatoes, curry sauce, tomatoes and cook, stirring, for 2–3 minutes.
3. Return the pork to the sauce, cover and simmer gently for 20 minutes or until the pork and potatoes are tender.
4. Remove from heat and stir in yoghurt and coriander. Serve hot with rice and naan bread.

Serves 4

Thai green pork curry

Pork mince does not require an egg to bind it, making it ideal for this curry. The curry pastes were launched around 2003 to meet New Zealanders' demand for flavoursome curries. They have continued to be a bold seller for Wattie's.

250–300 grams 100% New Zealand Trim Pork Mince
1 tblsp chopped coriander (optional)
1–2 tsp minced ginger
80 gram pouch Curry Creations Thai Green Curry Paste
½ cup salt-reduced chicken or vegetable stock
½ cup coconut milk or light coconut cream
1–2 cups torn spinach leaves (fresh or frozen), or green beans (fresh or frozen)

1. Mix together the pork mince with the coriander and ginger. Roll the mixture into walnut-sized balls.

2. Brown the pork balls in a dash of oil in a lidded frying pan.

3. Add the curry paste and cook for 1 minute until bubbling.

4. Stir in the stock and coconut milk and when hot add the meatballs. Turn to coat, then cover and simmer for 10 minutes. Stir in the spinach or green beans, cover and simmer for a further 3–4 minutes until the vegetables are cooked.

5. Serve over boiled white rice garnished with toasted coconut and coriander or sliced chilli.

Serves 2

Autumn vegetables and bean korma curry

Canned beans are usually thought of as a base for salads, but they are far more versatile than that. Here I used them for the protein ingredient in a delicious vegetarian curry.

2 onions, peeled and thickly sliced
2 tblsp oil
1 large orange-fleshed kumara, peeled and diced
½ cauliflower, cut into florets
1 cup water or vegetable stock
1 green pepper, diced
425 gram can Craig's Four Bean Mix in Brine, well drained
410 gram can Wattie's Korma Curry Sauce
½ cup plain unsweetened yoghurt or coconut milk
fresh coriander or mint to garnish (optional)

1. Cook the onions in the oil in a large lidded frying pan for 3–5 minutes or until the onions begin to soften.
2. Add the kumara, cauliflower and water or vegetable stock. Cover and simmer for 10 minutes.
3. Stir in the diced pepper, bean mix and curry sauce. Stir, cover and simmer for a further 10 minutes or until the vegetables are tender.
4. Stir in the yoghurt or coconut milk and season with salt and freshly ground pepper. Serve the curry over rice garnished with chopped coriander or mint if wished.

Serves 4

Lentil and vegetable butter curry

Lentils are an excellent source of vegetable protein, fibre and B vitamins and with them now canned under the Craig's label (so they're pre-cooked), they are easy to add to dishes such as this curry. Also mix into casseroles, pies and even a family meatloaf.

- 1 onion, peeled and diced
- 750 grams winter root vegetables (pumpkin, carrots, parsnips, potatoes and kumara)*
- 405 gram can Wattie's Butter Chicken Curry Sauce
- ½ cup water
- 100 grams green beans, trimmed and sliced
- 400 gram can Craig's Lentils in Brine, well rinsed and drained
- 2 tblsp cream
- 2 tblsp chopped fresh coriander or parsley

1. Brown the onion in a dash of oil in a deep lidded frying pan. Peel and dice the vegetables, add to the pan and toss quickly.
2. Stir in the curry sauce and water. Cover and simmer for 15 minutes.
3. Scatter over the beans and lentils. Cover and simmer for a further 5–8 minutes or until the vegetables are tender.
4. Stir in the cream and coriander or parsley. Serve rolled in Indian naan bread or flour tortillas and accompany with rice, or serve as part of an Indian meal.

Serves 4

*750 grams is equal to about 1 medium-sized carrot, parsnip, potato and kumara.

Curried winter vegetables

As households become busier, Wattie's are always looking for ways to cut down preparation time in the kitchen. This frozen vegetable mix with potatoes, carrots and kumara, all peeled and diced, is a great idea. Keep them on hand to add to casseroles and curries.

1 tsp each cumin seeds, fennel seeds and mustard seeds
2 tblsp oil
1 tsp ground turmeric
½–1 tsp salt
750 gram bag Wattie's Frozen Winter Veges Recipe Mix

1. Cook the whole spices in the oil in a frying pan for about 1 minute or until fragrant.

2. Stir in the turmeric and salt and then add the frozen vegetables. Toss quickly, adding a little water. Cover and steam for 4–5 minutes until tender and hot, stirring occasionally.

Serves 4–5

Tomato and bean salad, page 162

Salads & vegetables

Caesar-style salad 156
French salad 157
Greek-style salad 157
Honey mustard and smoked chicken pasta salad 158
Russian salad 159
Smoked chicken and melon salad 160
Warm chicken, grape and herb salad 160
Tomato and bean salad 162
Kumara and corned beef salad 163
Tropical baked kumara 164
Warm potato and bacon salad 165

Caesar-style salad

A classic Caesar salad dressing includes vinaigrette, Worcestershire sauce, lemon juice and usually anchovies. It has a deliciously tangy taste that jangles the taste buds and works so well with summer's crisp salad ingredients. How fabulous it is that Wattie's makes this — all the hard work is done for you!

1 iceberg lettuce, washed
2–3 thick slices crusty bread
4–6 rashers bacon, rind removed
3 tblsp oil or about 50 grams butter (garlic butter is nice here)
3 hard-boiled eggs, peeled and quartered
Eta Caesar Salad Dressing

1. Cut the iceberg lettuce into chunky pieces and arrange on a serving platter.
2. Cut the bread into large crouton-sized dice and chop the bacon roughly. Cook in the oil in a hot frying pan, tossing until the bacon and croutons are crisp. (Or melt the garlic butter in an ovenproof pan or roasting dish, add the bacon and bread and cook at 180°C until the bacon and bread are crisp.)
3. Scatter the cooled bacon and croutons on top of the lettuce with the hard-boiled eggs.
4. Pour plenty of dressing over the salad and serve.

Serves 4–6

French salad

A classic salad made with summer-time pantry store items.

500 gram bag Wattie's Frozen Broad Beans (optional)
½ x 500 gram bag Wattie's Frozen Whole Baby Beans
1 iceburg lettuce
4 tomatoes, sliced
10 cooked baby potatoes, halved
4 hard-boiled eggs
185 gram can Wattie's Tuna in Spring Water
12 black olives (optional)

Dressing
½ cup Eta Mayonnaise
¼ cup chopped fresh herbs
2 tblsp water

1. Blanch the broad and baby beans in boiling water for 2 minutes. Refresh in cold water, drain well. Peel the broad beans.
2. Wash and drain the lettuce. Cut into large pieces and arrange on a large platter.
3. Sprinkle over half the whole baby and broad beans. Top with the tomatoes and potatoes.
4. Halve the hard-boiled eggs and place on top. Sprinkle over the remaining whole baby and broad beans.
5. Drain the tuna and place pieces over the top of the salad. Lastly sprinkle over the olives.
6. Blend all the dressing ingredients together until smooth and spoon over just before serving.

Serves 5–6

Greek-style salad

3–4 cups baby spinach leaves, rinsed and drained
2–3 tomatoes, cut into wedges
100 grams feta cheese, cubed
300 gram can Craig's Chickpeas in Brine, rinsed and drained
½ red onion, peeled and sliced
¼ cup Italian parsley leaves
8 black olives
½ cup Eta Salad Times French Vinaigrette

1. Toss together the spinach leaves, tomatoes, feta, chickpeas, onion, parsley leaves, olives and French vinaigrette, and serve immediately.

Serves 4

Honey mustard and smoked chicken pasta salad

Often the easier the salads, the simpler the flavours and the nicer they are. These two recipes appeared in 2005, showcasing new chickpeas and the revamped Eta dressings.

400 grams pasta bows or penne
1 Tegel Smoked Chicken
3 spring onions, trimmed and sliced
150 grams grapes, halved
3–4 sticks celery, sliced finely
1–2 tblsp chopped fresh fennel, dill or basil
grated rind 1 lemon
1 cup Eta Salad Times Honey Mustard Dressing

1. Cook pasta in boiling salted water for 12 minutes or until tender, drain and rinse in cold water to stop the cooking. Drain well.
2. Pull the chicken into bite-sized pieces, removing the skin.
3. Toss together the pasta, smoked chicken pieces, spring onions, grapes, celery, herbs, lemon rind and mustard dressing.

Serves 4–5

Russian salad

Salads have grown from a side dish (when we first began Food in a Minute) to a substantial meal, either lunch or dinner. This simple recipe can be altered using different spicy sausages or different lettuces.

6 spicy sausages
½ x 750 gram bag Wattie's Frozen Whole Baby Beans
1 buttercrunch or butterhead lettuce
4 tomatoes, diced
10 cooked baby potatoes, halved
4 hard-boiled eggs, peeled and halved
1 each red and green pepper, sliced
820 gram can Wattie's Whole Baby Beetroot, well drained

Dressing
¼ cup each orange juice, honey, oil and cider vinegar
¼ chopped fresh herbs (parsley, chives, lemon, thyme, etc)

1. Cook the sausages in a frying pan or under the grill. Allow to cool. Cut into slices on the diagonal.

2. Blanch the baby beans and refresh in cold water. Drain well on absorbent paper.

3. Wash and drain the lettuce leaves. Arrange on a large salad plate.

4. Sprinkle over the whole baby beans, tomatoes, potatoes, eggs and half the peppers.

5. Halve any large beetroot and arrange neatly on top with the sliced sausage and remaining peppers.

6. To make the dressing blend all ingredients together until smooth and spoon over salad just before serving.

Serves 4

Smoked chicken and melon salad

When this recipe went to air in mid-2003 we were inundated with requests for the recipe for weeks and weeks. It tastes great and it is one of my all-time Food in a Minute summer favourites.

1 Tegel Smoked Chicken or 2 Tegel Smoked Chicken Breast Fillets
½ cantaloupe (rock melon)
½ honeydew melon
2–3 tomatoes
½ –¾ cup Eta Mayonnaise
2–3 tblsp pesto
¼ cup chopped fresh parsley or basil leaves

1. Pull the meat from the whole chicken. Cut or pull the smoked chicken meat into bite-sized pieces. If using chicken breast fillets, cut into bite-sized pieces.

2. Scoop the seeds from the melons and cut away the skin. Dice or slice the melons into 2 cm pieces.

3. Cut the tomatoes into thin wedges.

4. Toss the smoked chicken, melon, tomatoes, mayonnaise and pesto together and arrange on a serving plate. Sprinkle over the parsley or basil.

Serves 4–6

Warm chicken, grape and herb salad

Another popular chicken salad, this time with juicy grapes and fragrent herbs.

1.5 kg Whole Tegel Chicken
½ lemon
1 tblsp oil
2 tblsp white wine vinegar
2 tblsp liquid honey
grated rind and juice 1 lemon
2–3 tblsp chopped fresh herbs
300 grams your favourite pasta shape
2–3 spring onions, sliced
100 grams green grapes, halved if large
3 sticks celery, thinly sliced

1. Wash the chicken, pat dry with absorbent paper, rub with half a cut lemon, inside and out. Roast at 180°C for about 1½ hours, or until cooked.

2. Prepare the dressing by mixing the oil, vinegar, honey, lemon rind and juice with freshly chopped herbs.

3. About 10 minutes before the chicken is cooked, cook the pasta in boiling, salted water until 'al dente'. Drain well.

4. Cut hot, cooked chicken into bite-sized pieces and toss with warm pasta, spring onion, grapes, celery and dressing. Serve immediately.

Serves 5–6

Left: Warm chicken, grape and herb salad
Right: Smoked chicken and melon salad

Tomato and bean salad

Our Food in a Minute food team were all very excited when Wattie's launched their own canned cannellini beans. They are nutritious and versatile and we launched them to market in a delicious salad. Other ways to use them include adding them to casseroles, soups and meatloaves.

300 grams very thick cut Kiwi bacon, finely diced
¼ cup cider vinegar
¼ cup honey
400 gram can Craig's Cannellini Beans, well rinsed and drained
½ large red onion, finely diced
12–16 black olives (juicy Kalamata olives are good)
¼ cup chopped fresh parsley or basil
400–500 grams tomatoes, thinly sliced

1. Pan-fry the bacon until very crisp. Pour in the cider vinegar and honey, and stir to release the sediment from under the bacon. Set aside.
2. In a bowl toss together the beans, red onion, olives, parsley or basil and the bacon and cider vinegar mixture. Season well with freshly ground black pepper.
3. Arrange the tomato slices around the edge of a platter. Pile the bean salad into the centre. Serve soon after making.

Serves 6

Kumara and corned beef salad

Here again is that much-loved combination of kumara and corned beef. This salad is also ideal made with the low-fat corned beef.

- 500 grams orange-fleshed kumara, peeled
- 2 oranges
- 340 gram can Hellaby's Corned Beef
- 3–4 spring onions, sliced
- ¼ cup mint leaves
- 227 gram can crushed pineapple, well drained
- ½ cup Eta Mayonnaise
- ¼ cup sour cream
- 1 tblsp wholeseed mustard

1. Cut the kumara into 3 cm chunks and simmer until tender. Drain and cool.
2. Grate the rind from the oranges. Cut away the pith and segment or dice the orange.
3. Cut the corned beef into dice and place in a bowl with the orange rind, orange flesh, spring onions, mint, pineapple, mayonnaise, sour cream and mustard. Season with salt and pepper and toss gently to mix.

Serves 4

Tropical baked kumara

Over the years of creating recipes for Food in a Minute we have found combinations that our viewers love and maybe prefer. Kumara and corned beef is one of those, so when we looked at doing something as simple as a baked potato, we made the television recipe with kumara and, yes, it was a smash hit back in 2004.

4 medium-sized orange or golden kumara
½ cup crushed pineapple, well drained
1 tsp minced fresh ginger (optional)
2–3 spring onions, trimmed and finely chopped
340 gram can Hellaby's Corned Beef
¼–½ cup cheddar cheese, grated

1. Wash the kumara and dry well. Trim the ends. Rub the kumara with oil and place on a baking tray. Cook at 200°C for 45–50 minutes or until well cooked. Alternatively prick the kumara with a fork and microwave on high power for 15 minutes or until tender.

2. Slice a top off each kumara and scoop the flesh into a bowl.

3. Add the pineapple, ginger (if using), spring onions and corned beef and mix gently with a fork to break up the corned beef and mix the ingredients lightly. Do not mash.

4. Refill each kumara with quarter of the mixture and return to the baking tray. Sprinkle each with a little cheese.

5. Cook at 200°C for 15 minutes until piping hot and golden.

Serves 4

Warm potato and bacon salad

Waxy potatoes stay whole when they are cooked, making them ideal for salads. Varieties include most early-season potatoes: Nadine, Draga, Jersey Bennes and Frisia. Serve the salad soon after it has been dressed as the potatoes will soak up the dressing far quicker when warm.

750 grams–1 kg waxy potatoes, peeled
4 rashers bacon, diced
½ cup Eta Warm Potato Salad Dressing
4–5 spring onions, trimmed and sliced
2 tblsp chopped fresh herbs (parsley, mint, tarragon, sage or oregano)

1. Cut the potatoes into thick slices and boil in salted water until tender. Alternatively, toss the slices in a dash of oil and roast at 200°C until cooked.

2. Cook the bacon in a hot frying pan until it is very crisp. Drain on absorbent paper.

3. Arrange the potatoes in a serving dish and dress with spoonfuls of the potato salad dressing. Scatter over the bacon, spring onions and herbs. Season with freshly ground black pepper and serve warm.

Serves 4

Three berry chocoholics cake, page 172

Desserts & baking

Blueberry chocolate cake	168
Boysenberry ripple cake with custard	169
Carrot and orange cake	170
Three berry chocoholics cake	172
Yoghurt and pear syrup cake	173
Apple muffins with spicy topping	174
Blueberry jam muffins	176
Creamy tropical muffins	177
No-fuss apple tart	178
Nutty banoffee pie	179
One crust fruit pie	180
Sour cream apple pie	182
Peanut slice	183
Summer peach and cream cheese slice	184
Creamy strawberry and amaretti dessert	185
Creamy boysenberry pudding	185
No-cook chocolate Christmas pudding	186
Queen rice pudding	188
Chocolate berry cheesecake	189
Orange and mango cheesecake ice-cream	190
Vanilla and boysenberry ice-cream cake	191
Quick trifle	192
Minted tropical fruit salad	193
Grilled bananas with apricot sauce	194
Black doris plum self-saucing pudding	196
Blackberry bread and butter pudding	197
Fruity blueberry self-saucing pudding	198
Boysenberry apple crumble	200
Tamarillo and boysenberry crumble	201
Marmalade steamed pudding	202

Blueberry chocolate cake

I particularly liked the glaze that accompanied this cake. The thick chocolate glaze pours over smoothly, covering the cake with an indulgent layer of smooth chocolate. This recipe first appeared around 2000.

½ cup cocoa
¾ cup water
250 grams butter, softened
1 cup brown sugar
1 tsp vanilla essence
3 eggs
375 gram jar Craig's Blueberry Jam
2½ cups self-raising flour
grated chocolate for decoration (optional)

1. Stir the cocoa and hot water together until smooth. Cool thoroughly.
2. Beat the butter, brown sugar and vanilla essence together until light and fluffy. Beat in the eggs one at a time, beating well after each addition. Beat in ½ cup of the jam.
3. Sift in the self-raising flour and pour in the cooled chocolate mixture. Fold together carefully. Spread into a well-greased and floured 22–23 cm ring cake tin.
4. Bake at 180°C for 40 minutes or until a skewer inserted comes out clean and the cake has shrunk from the sides of the cake tin. Cool in the cake tin for 5 minutes before turning out on to a cake rack to cool.
5. When cool, split the cake in half or three layers horizontally and spread the cut layers with the remaining jam. Join together. Dust with icing sugar or spread with Thick Chocolate Glaze and a little grated chocolate for decoration.

Thick chocolate glaze

Microwave 125 grams chocolate chips and ¼ cup cream (plain or sour) in a microwave-proof jug for 1 minute on high power. Stir until the chocolate has all melted and the mixture is smooth.

Makes 1 cake

Boysenberry ripple cake with custard

Rather than always icing a cake, top it with a crunchy oat crumble for texture and appearance and, if you wish, dust with a little icing sugar before serving.

125 grams butter, softened
1 cup castor sugar
1 egg
1½ cups self-raising flour
2 tsp ground cinnamon
1 tsp mixed spice
¼ tsp salt
425 gram can Wattie's Boysenberries in Syrup, well drained
½ cup milk

½ cup brown sugar
25 grams butter, melted
½ cup rolled oats
1 tsp mixed spice

1. Beat the butter and sugar together until light and creamy. Add the egg and beat well.
2. Sift the flour, cinnamon, mixed spice and salt together and fold into the creamed mixture with the boysenberries and milk.
3. Turn into a lightly greased and floured 20 cm cake tin.
4. Mix together the brown sugar, melted butter, rolled oats and spice and sprinkle over the cake.
5. Bake at 180°C for 40–45 minutes until cooked when tested with a skewer. Cool on a cake rack and serve with warm custard.

Makes 1 cake

Carrot and orange cake

Buttermilk will give this carrot cake a refreshing flavour with a moist texture. For those watching their weight, I suggest you use only half the icing.

1 cup oil
1 cup dark brown sugar
2 eggs
1 tblsp vanilla essence
grated rind 2 oranges
2 cups carrot, grated
½ cup sultanas
3 cups flour
1 tblsp mixed spice
2 tsp baking powder
1 tsp baking soda
1 cup Tararua Cultured Buttermilk

Icing
250 gram pottle Tararua Cream Cheese
1 cup icing sugar, sifted
dash vanilla essence

1. In a large bowl beat together the oil, sugar, eggs, vanilla essence and orange rind. Once well beaten, stir in the grated carrot and sultanas.

2. Sift the flour, spice, baking powder and soda together and gently stir into the carrot mixture with the buttermilk. Transfer to a well-greased and lined 23 cm cake tin.

3. Bake at 160°C for 60–70 minutes until a skewer inserted comes out clean. Cool in the tin for 10 minutes before turning out onto a cake rack to cool.

4. Beat the cream cheese with the icing sugar and vanilla essence until smooth.

5. Split the cake in half horizontally and spread with half the cream cheese icing. Top with the remaining cake and spread with the remaining cream cheese icing. If wished, decorate with grated orange rind.

Serves 8–10

Three berry chocoholics cake

Berries have a natural synergy with chocolate and that's why we often pair them together on Food in a Minute.

1 cup chocolate chips
1 cup whole milk
125 grams butter, softened
½ cup brown sugar
½ cup Craig's Three Berry Jam
2 eggs
2 cups self-raising flour
icing sugar to dust
whipped cream to serve

Three Berry Sauce
Craig's Three Berry Jam (remaining jam left in the jar)
¼ cup hot water

1. Melt the chocolate chips in the milk in the microwave on high power for about 4–5 minutes. Stir to melt the chocolate chips, then cool thoroughly.

2. Beat the butter and sugar together until light and creamy, and beat in the jam. Add the eggs, one at a time, beating well after each addition.

3. Sift the flour and fold into the creamed mixture with the cooled chocolate mix. Turn into a well-greased and lined 23 cm cake tin.

4. Bake at 180°C for 35–40 minutes until a skewer inserted comes out clean. Stand for 10 minutes before turning out onto a cake rack to cool.

5. Mix the remaining jam with the hot water and then sieve. Dust the cake with icing sugar and serve in wedges, with a dollop of whipped cream and a little Three Berry Sauce to accompany.

Serves 8–10

Yoghurt and pear syrup cake

Simply delicious. This recipe is based on one of my all-time favourite cake recipes. Semolina adds a mild grainy texture; if you do not have any, add extra flour. Ideal as a pudding or a special afternoon tea cake.

250 grams butter, softened
1 cup castor sugar
grated rind 2 lemons
4 eggs
2½–3 cups self-raising flour
½ cup semolina
1 cup Naturalea Plain Unsweetened Yoghurt
410 gram can Wattie's Pear Quarters in Juice, drained and juice reserved
reserved pear juice
about ¼ cup lemon juice
½ cup sugar

1. Beat the butter, castor sugar and lemon rind together until light and fluffy. Add eggs, one at a time, beating well after each addition.

2. Sift the flour and fold into the creamed mixture. Add the semolina and yoghurt.

3. Turn into a lightly greased and lined 24 cm cake tin. Arrange the pears evenly on top.

4. Bake at 180°C for 1¼ hours until golden and the cake is cooked when tested with a skewer.

5. Make the reserved pear juice up to 1 cup with lemon juice, place in a saucepan and heat with the sugar until dissolved.

6. Once the cake is cooked, leave in tin, pierce the top with a bamboo skewer and slowly pour over the syrup. Allow to cool in the tin for 1 hour before turning out. Serve with extra yoghurt on the side.

Serves 8

Apple muffins with spicy topping

This recipe, featuring back in the late 1990s, is a basic muffin recipe jazzed up with a sugar and spice topping. Vary the recipe with different Wattie's fruits such as peaches or nectarines.

3 cups flour
2 tblsp baking powder
¾ cup castor sugar
1 tsp each ground ginger and mixed spice
2 eggs
380 gram can Wattie's Diced Apple
1½ cups milk
few drops vanilla essence
100 grams melted butter, cooled
16 walnut halves (optional)

juice of one lemon
1 tsp each castor sugar and mixed spice, mixed together

1. Sift the flour, baking powder, castor sugar and spices into a bowl.
2. Mix together the eggs, apple, milk and vanilla essence. Make a well in the centre of the bowl and pour in the apple and milk mixture. Stir gently with a holed spoon until the batter is just mixed. Fold through the butter.
3. Do not over-mix the batter mixture as the muffins will peak like Mt Everest. Lift the mixture up with the spoon and turn it over on top of the remaining mix in the bowl. Give the bowl a quarter turn and then repeat this lifting and mixing routine until all ingredients are just blended.
4. Three-quarters fill 16 well-greased muffin tins. Decorate each muffin with a walnut half, if using.
5. Bake at 220°C for about 15–20 minutes until well risen, golden and cooked.
6. Remove from the oven and wait 2–3 minutes. Mix together the sugar and mixed spice for the topping. Brush the tops of the muffins with the lemon juice. Sprinkle over the mixed spice sugar.

Makes 16

Blueberry jam muffins

This recipe appeared in May 2006, helping us to celebrate 10 years of Food in a Minute. It's great to know that favourite recipes such as muffins are still as popular as when we started.

2 cups self-raising flour
½ cup castor sugar
1 egg, lightly beaten
¾ cup milk
1 tsp vanilla essence
100 grams butter, melted
1 tblsp golden syrup
6 tblsp Craig's Blueberry Jam
¼ cup cream cheese

1. Sift the flour and sugar into a bowl and make a well in the centre.

2. Mix egg, milk and vanilla essence together. Stir in to the dry ingredients with the melted butter and golden syrup.

3. Half-fill 12 well-greased muffin tins, place a heaped teaspoon of jam and a teaspoon cream cheese into the centre of each muffin. Carefully cover the jam with the remaining muffin mixture.

3. Bake at 220°C for 12–15 minutes, or until golden and firm to the touch.

4. Cool in the tin for 5 minutes. Serve warm, dusted with icing sugar.

Makes 12

Creamy tropical muffins

These muffins appeared in Food in a Minute Book 3 in 1999, when any muffin containing bran was incredibly popular. The combination of tropical fruits adds a refreshing flavour and the yoghurt helps ensure a tender muffin.

2 cups flour
1 tsp baking soda
2 tsp baking powder
½ cup sugar
1 cup bran
425 gram can Wattie's Tropical Fruit Salad in Juice
1 egg
¾ cup fruit salad yoghurt
grated rind 2 oranges or lemons
100 grams butter, melted
about ½ cup cream cheese

1. Sift the flour, baking soda, baking powder and sugar into a bowl. Stir in the bran.

2. Put the fruit chunks with the juice, egg, yoghurt and orange or lemon rind into a food processor and process until evenly and finely chopped.

3. Pour the fruit into the dry ingredients and fold together with the butter.

4. Half-fill 12 well-greased muffin tins. Place a teaspoon of cream cheese in the centre of each and top with the remaining muffin mixture.

5. Bake at 220°C for 15–18 minutes until well risen and golden. Cool in the tin for 5 minutes before serving.

Makes 12

No-fuss apple tart

Of all the recipes I have created or presented, this remains my personal all-time favourite. If you're a guest in my home, odds are this is the pudding you'll be served. I often change the fruit using canned or home-cooked, whatever's on hand. This original recipe calls for flour and baking powder but use self-raising flour if you have it on hand.

250 grams very soft butter (but not melted)
¾ cup castor sugar
1 egg
grated rind of 1 orange
1 tsp vanilla essence
2½ cups flour
2½ tsp baking powder
380 gram can Wattie's Diced Apple
icing sugar to serve with

1. In a bowl or food processor beat together the butter, castor sugar, egg, orange rind and vanilla essence until creamy and well mixed.
2. Add the flour and baking powder and stir or pulse to mix well.
3. Spread two-thirds of the mixture into the base of a well greased and floured 23 cm loose cake tin.
4. Spread over the apple.
5. With floured hands dot the remaining dough over the top.
6. Bake at 190°C for 40 minutes. When cool dust with icing sugar and serve with whipped cream.

Serves 6–8

Nutty banoffee pie

Definitely one of the over-the-top, but ever-so-delicious desserts.

2 sheets defrosted, pre-rolled sweet short pastry
75 grams butter
½ cup firmly packed brown sugar
250 gram pottle Tararua Traditional Cream Cheese
½–¾ cup Eta Smooth Peanut Butter
1 egg
3 bananas, peeled
whipped cream and grated chocolate (optional)

1. Roll the 2 sheets of short pastry together until they are large enough to line the base and sides of a 24 cm loose-bottom flan tin. Trim the edges.
2. Line the pastry with baking paper and fill with baking blind material.
3. Bake at 190°C for 12 minutes, and then remove the baking blind material and return the flan to the oven for a further 5–7 minutes until the pastry is well cooked. Cool.
4. Put the butter and sugar in a saucepan and when the butter has melted, simmer for 1 minute.
5. Stir in the cream cheese and peanut butter and continue to stir until the mixture is smooth and thick. Quickly beat in the egg. Remove from heat.
6. Slice the bananas over the base of the pastry flan, then pour over the peanut toffee filling. Refrigerate for 2 hours or until required. Serve plain or topped with whipped cream. If wished, garnish with grated chocolate.

Serves 8–10

One crust fruit pie

Bananas are a household staple fruit, so I included them here for their flavour and goodness. They will brown during cooking but remain delicious to eat.

2 cups flour
175 grams butter
2–4 tblsp sugar
3–4 tblsp cold water

820 gram can Wattie's Peach Slices in Syrup or Juice, well drained
2 bananas, peeled and sliced
2 tblsp honey
2 tblsp cornflour
milk to glaze
2 tblsp extra sugar
icing sugar for dusting

1. Sift the flour into a bowl. Rub in the butter until it resembles crumbs. Stir in the sugar. Use a knife to cut in sufficient cold water to make a firm dough.

2. Turn out onto a floured board and knead lightly. Roll out to a 30 cm-diameter round. Transfer to a greased baking tray.

3. Toss the peaches, bananas, honey and cornflour together and pile into the centre of the pastry.

4. Flip the edges of the pastry over, leaving the middle of the tart uncovered. Brush the edges with milk to glaze and sprinkle with the extra sugar.

5. Bake towards the top of the oven at 200°C for 30–35 minutes until hot and golden. Dust with icing sugar to serve.

Serves 6

Sour cream apple pie

Wattie's apple products are always on my pantry shelf. They are just blanched apples, canned. Cooking with apples is made so much easier by using these products.

2 cups flour
¼ cup sugar
175 grams chilled butter
2–3 tblsp water
820 gram can Wattie's Sliced Apple
½ cup sour cream
1 egg
grated rind one lemon
milk to glaze
icing sugar for dusting

1. Put the flour, sugar and butter into a food processor and process until the mixture resembles fine crumbs.
2. Pour sufficient water down the feed tube and pulse until the mixture resembles small moist balls of dough.
3. Turn out and bring together. Roll out to a 30 cm round and place over the base and sides of a 24 cm flan tin.
4. In a bowl mix together the apple slices, sour cream, egg and lemon rind and pour into the centre of the pastry-lined tin.
5. Flip the edges over and brush them with milk to glaze. The edges are not meant to cover the filling completely.
6. Bake at 190°C for 35–40 minutes until the pastry is golden.
7. Dust with icing sugar before serving.

Serves 6–8

Peanut slice

What is a childhood without peanut butter? This is an ideal lunchbox slice for hungry teenagers.

200 grams butter, softened
1 cup sugar
1 egg
2 cups flour
½ tsp baking powder
397 gram can sweetened condensed milk
2 tblsp golden syrup
375 gram jar Eta Smooth or Crunchy Peanut Butter

1. Beat the butter and sugar together until the mixture is pale in colour and light in texture. Add the egg and beat well.

2. Sift in the flour and baking powder and mix to form a soft dough. Press three-quarters of the dough onto the base of a baking paper-lined, 20 cm x 30 cm slice tin.

3. In a saucepan warm the condensed milk and golden syrup. Stir in the peanut butter. Spread evenly over the base of the slice. Dot the remaining dough over the top of the peanut layer.

4. Bake at 180°C for 30–35 minutes until the slice is golden. Cool in the tin before cutting into slices to serve. Keep in an airtight container.

Makes 30 pieces

Summer peach and cream cheese slice

This dessert is like a fruit-layered cheesecake cooked on top of a shortcake base. Ideal for entertaining.

100 grams softened butter
¾ cup sugar
2 eggs
1½ cups self-raising flour
½ cup desiccated coconut
¼ cup milk

820 gram can Wattie's Peach Slices in Juice, well drained
250 gram pottle cream cheese
¼ cup sugar
1 egg
dash of vanilla essence (optional)

1. Place the butter, sugar, eggs, flour, coconut and milk into a food processor and process until just blended.
2. Spread mixture into a greased and lined 24 cm x 30 cm slice tin.
3. Arrange the peach slices randomly or in neat, even rows on top.
4. Blend the cream cheese, sugar, egg and vanilla essence together in the food processor and pour over the top of the peaches.
5. Bake at 190°C for 20–25 minutes until golden and well risen. Serve in slices.

Serves 6–8

Creamy strawberry and amaretti dessert

Amaretti biscuits are brittle almond macaroons. If you cannot find them in your supermarket, use 12 shortbread-style biscuits.

250 gram pottle Meadow Fresh Sweetened Thickened Cream
125 gram pottle Meadow Fresh Strawberry Yoghurt
½ punnet strawberries, hulled and quartered
extra strawberries to garnish
12 amaretti biscuits, crushed

1. In a bowl stir together the cream and yoghurt.
2. Fold in the strawberries and crushed amaretti biscuits.
3. Spoon the mixture into individual glasses to serve and top with extra strawberries. Serve immediately.

Serves 3–4

Creamy boysenberry pudding

Use unsweetened yoghurt here for a lovely pudding.

½ cup cream
420 gram can Wattie's 99% Fat Free Vanilla Creamed Rice
1 cup Naturalea Plain Unsweetened Yoghurt
180 gram packet marshmallows, halved
425 gram can Wattie's Boysenberries in Syrup, well drained

1. Whip the cream until it forms soft peaks.
2. In a bowl fold together the creamed rice, yoghurt, marshmallows, boysenberries and whipped cream.
3. Pile into individual serving glasses or 1 large bowl. Refrigerate for 1–2 hours before serving.

Serves 6–8

No-cook chocolate Christmas pudding

Mainland's chocolate mousse ensured our dessert recipe for Christmas 2004 was incredibly successful. For best results make this pudding 24 hours ahead of serving. This way it will cut easily into portions.

20 cm double round plain sponge, halved horizontally
4 tblsp orange liqueur or orange juice
500 gram pottle Tararua Chocolate Mousse
½ cup roasted hazelnuts, coarsely chopped
½ cup roughly chopped dried apricots
½ cup Meadow Fresh Sweetened Thickened Cream
½ cup chopped dark chocolate
½ cup mixed peel
cocoa and icing sugar to dust

1. Line the inside of a large bowl with plastic wrap. Cut the sponge into triangular slices 1.5 cm thick. Brush one side of the cake slices with orange liqueur or juice and use to line the bowl, placing the narrow end of the cake slices in the centre of the base. Reserve leftover cake for the top.

2. Beat the chocolate mousse until it doubles in volume and stir in the hazelnuts and apricots. Spread into the bowl, leaving a cavity in the centre.

3. Mix the cream with the chocolate chips and mixed peel and use to fill the cavity. Use the leftover cake to cover the top. Cover with plastic wrap and refrigerate overnight. If possible, place a weight on top. Turn out and dust with cocoa and icing sugar.

Serves 6–8

Queen rice pudding

As a girl, my mother often added leftover cooked rice to a baked pudding. It stretched the pudding further and added additional nutrition. This recipe was based loosely on my mother's. Creamed rice is incredibly versatile and makes a great base for quick desserts.

420 gram can Wattie's Original Creamy Vanilla Creamed Rice
1 cup milk
2 eggs
2 egg yolks
¼ cup castor sugar
4 tblsp Craig's Raspberry Jam
2 egg whites

1. With a fork, mix together the creamed rice, milk, whole eggs, egg yolks and half the sugar. Pour into 4 well-greased 1-cup capacity sturdy teacups or ramekins.

2. Place the cups in a large baking dish and take to the oven. Fill the baking dish with sufficient water to come one-third of the way up the sides of the cups. Bake at 180°C for 25–30 minutes until the custard has set in the cups or ramekins.

3. Carefully remove from the oven. Spread each cup with one tablespoonful of jam.

4. In a clean bowl beat the egg whites until stiff peaks form and then beat in the remaining sugar until the mixture is fluffy and meringue-like.

5. Pile one-quarter of the mixture on each baked custard. Return to the oven for 5 minutes. Stand 5 minutes before serving.

Serves 4

Chocolate berry cheesecake

Ideal for summer, this recipe featured co-sponsor Mainland's new cheesecake mix, which sells out each time the product appears on Food in a Minute. It seems Kiwis are cheesecake fans through and through.

250 grams sweet plain chocolate biscuits
100 grams butter, melted
425 gram can Wattie's Boysenberries in Syrup
500 gram pottle Tararua Cheesecake Mix
2 tsp gelatine

1. Crush the biscuits in a food processor or by placing in a sealed plastic bag and crushing with a rolling pin. Stir in the melted butter. Press into the base and sides of a 23 cm loose-bottom flan tin. Refrigerate until required.

2. Drain and reserve the juice from the boysenberries.

3. Beat together the drained boysenberries and cheesecake mix until smooth. Spread into the prepared flan. Refrigerate for 1 hour before serving like this or, if you like, top with the boysenberry glaze.

4. Sprinkle the gelatine over the reserved boysenberry juice and when it has been absorbed, warm the mixture in the microwave for 2 minutes on high and stir until dissolved. Cool. Pour over the chilled cheesecake and refrigerate a further hour before serving.

Serves 6

Orange and mango cheesecake ice-cream

To ensure this ice-cream is creamy when frozen, use traditional cream cheese. Add the juice of 2–3 passionfruit for a tropical flavour.

- 2 x 250 gram pottles cream cheese
- grated rind and juice of 2 oranges
- 425 gram can Wattie's Mango Slices in Syrup, well drained
- 2 eggs
- 2 egg yolks
- ¾ cup castor sugar

1. Process the cream cheese, orange rind and juice and mangoes in a food processor until the cream cheese is very smooth and the mangoes puréed.

2. In a clean bowl mix together the eggs, egg yolks and castor sugar until the mixture is very thick and pale lemon in colour.

3. Add the egg mixture to the cream mixture and pulse to combine. Alternatively, fold together with a slotted spoon.

4. Pour into a wide, plastic wrap-lined, 6-cup capacity loaf tin. Cover with foil and freeze overnight or until solid.

5. Serve in scoops or slices with tropical fruit salad or fresh fruits.

Serves 6–8

Vanilla and boysenberry ice-cream cake

Canned fruit is often a cupboard standby, and with a tub of ice-cream we created this hugely popular dessert that required only a few additional ingredients. Appearing on Food in a Minute on television in the first 12 months, it still remains a popular recipe on our website.

2 litres Tip Top Vanilla Ice-cream
300 ml bottle cream
½ cup icing sugar
425 gram can Wattie's Boysenberries in Syrup, well drained
½ cup chocolate chips
2 tblsp cocoa for dusting

1. Spread half the ice-cream into the base of a paper-lined 23 cm loose-bottom cake tin. Place in the freezer. Place the remaining ice-cream back into the freezer.
2. Whip the cream and icing sugar together until very thick. Fold in the boysenberries and chocolate chips.
3. Spread the boysenberry cream over the base of the ice-cream in the cake tin. Return to the freezer for 2 hours.
4. Spread the remaining ice-cream over the boysenberry cream and return to the freezer for at least six hours and preferably overnight.
5. To serve, warm a cloth and run around the outside of the cake tin. Remove the sides of the cake tin and place the ice-cream cake onto a serving plate. Dust with cocoa and cut into wedges to serve.

Serves 8–10

Quick trifle

The ideal pudding for a summer barbecue.

1 half of a double sponge
about 4 tblsp Craig's Raspberry Jam
½ cup sweet or medium-sweet sherry
410 gram can Wattie's Fruit Salad in Light Syrup, well drained
300 ml bottle cream
600 ml carton prepared vanilla custard
¼ cup grated chocolate

1. Spread sponge with the raspberry jam and place in the base and sides of a large serving bowl.
2. Pour over the sherry. (A splash more won't hurt.)
3. Spread the well-drained fruit salad on top.
4. Whip the cream until stiff and stir half the whipped cream with the custard. Spread the custard evenly over the fruit and sponge.
5. Spread the remaining whipped cream over the top of the custard and refrigerate one hour before serving. Decorate with grated chocolate before serving.

Serves 8

Minted tropical fruit salad

Using Wattie's tropcial fruit chunks as a base for this refreshing and healthy fruit salad makes life very easy. Add a little mint and grated lime and the finished dessert is perfect on a hot day.

2 x 425 gram cans Wattie's Tropical Fruit Salad in Syrup
2 bananas
¼ watermelon
2 tblsp finely chopped mint
grated rind and juice of 2 limes or lemons

1. Drain the fruit salad chunks and reserve the syrup.
2. Peel and cut the bananas into 1–2 cm thick slices. Cut the watermelon into 2cm chunks.
3. Mix the reserved syrup, mint, lime or lemon rind and juice together.
4. In a large bowl mix together the fruit salad, bananas, watermelon and syrup. Toss gently to coat. Cover and refrigerate for 30 minutes before serving.

Serves 6

Grilled bananas with apricot sauce

Bananas are one of our most popular weekly purchases. Here they are served grilled on skewers with apricot sauce for a quick fruit dessert.

410 gram can Wattie's Apricot Halves in Clear Juice
4 bananas
1 tblsp butter
2–3 tblsp brown sugar
pinch mixed spice (optional)
plain yoghurt or whipped cream to accompany

1. Puree the apricots with their juice or syrup and set aside.

2. Peel the bananas and cut into thick 2 cm slices. Place 4–5 slices on bamboo skewers.

3. Heat the butter in a non-stick frying pan and cook the bananas for 2–3 minutes, turning until golden.

4. Add the brown sugar and mixed spice if using, toss over the heat until the sugar has melted and glazed the bananas. Serve with the apricot sauce and yoghurt or whipped cream.

Serves 4

Black doris plum self-saucing pudding

At home my family's meals still include puddings, especially in winter when we enjoy them snuggled up by the fire on a late weeknight. Self-saucing puddings in any guise are always a favourite, as this one seemed to be when it went to air in 1998.

2 cups self-raising flour
¼ cup sugar
100 grams butter
1 egg
1 cup milk
1 tsp vanilla essence
375 gram jar Craig's Black Doris Plum Jam
1 cup boiling water

1. Sift the flour and sugar into a bowl.
2. Rub in the butter until the mixture resembles coarse crumbs.
3. Blend the egg, milk and vanilla essence together and pour into the dry ingredients. Mix together gently.
4. Spread the batter over the base of a well-greased, 2-litre capacity pie dish.
5. Mix the plum jam with the boiling water and pour carefully over the top of the batter.
6. Bake at 180°C for 35–45 minutes until the pudding is golden and well risen.
7. Stand for 5 minutes before serving, as the sauce is very hot. Serve hot with whipped cream.

Serves 6

Blackberry bread and butter pudding

A delicious variation on a classic favourite.

7–8 thick slices crusty bread
50 grams butter, softened
375 gram jar Craig's Blackberry Jam
250 gram pottle Tararua Crème Fraîche
4 large or 5 small eggs
½ cup sugar
1–2 tsp finely grated orange rind
2½ cups whole milk

Blackberry sauce
¼ cup Craig's Blackberry Jam
¼ cup orange juice

1. Spread the bread slices evenly with the butter and half a cup of the jam. Make into sandwiches and cut into quarters diagonally. Arrange in a greased ovenproof baking dish.

2. Beat the crème fraîche with the eggs, castor sugar and orange rind until thick and creamy. Gradually add the milk before gently pouring over the bread.

3. Bake in a water bath at 180°C for about 1 hour or until the custard is set. Serve warm with blackberry sauce.

4. To make the blackberry sauce, gently heat the jam with the orange juice, do not boil. Sieve to remove the seeds before serving if wished.

Serves 6–7

Fruity blueberry self-saucing pudding

In case you're out of blueberries, this delicious pudding can be made with raspberries and Craig's Raspberry Jam.

2 cups self-raising flour
¼ cup sugar
100 grams butter
1 egg
1 cup milk
grated rind one lemon
1½ cups fresh or frozen blueberries

375 gram jar Craig's Blueberry Jam
1 cup boiling water

1. Sift the flour and sugar into a bowl. Rub in the butter until the mixture forms coarse crumbs.

2. Blend the egg and milk together and pour into the dry ingredients. Mix together gently.

3. Scatter the blueberries over the base of a well-greased 2-litre capacity pie dish. Dot the batter on top.

4. Mix the Craig's Blueberry Jam with the hot water and pour carefully over the top of the batter.

5. Bake at 180°C for 40–45 minutes until the pudding is golden and well risen. Stand for 5 minutes before serving as the sauce is very hot.

Serves 4–6

Boysenberry apple crumble

Crumbles are a time-honoured favourite Kiwi pudding. It's the delicious combination of a buttery crumble with luscious sweet fruit hidden underneath that we all seem to enjoy in winter. Using jam helped add summer flavours to this recipe. As always, this classic pudding was extremely popular with our viewers.

770 gram can Wattie's Sliced Apple
¾ cup Craig's Boysenberry Jam
1 cup flour
½ cup brown sugar
1 cup rolled oats
1–2 tsp ground cinnamon or cardamom
70 gram packet slivered almonds, optional
150 grams butter, melted
3 tblsp Craig's Boysenberry Jam
1 cup Naturalea Plain Unsweetened Yoghurt

1. Mix apple and jam together and turn into a deep ovenproof dish.
2. In a bowl combine flour, brown sugar, rolled oats, cinnamon or cardamom and almonds. Stir in the butter until well combined.
3. Spoon over boysenberry apple mixture.
4. Cook at 180°C for 35–40 minutes or until crisp and golden.
5. Swirl jam into the yoghurt and serve with the crumble.

Serves 6

Tamarillo and boysenberry crumble

Heinz Wattie's owns the Weight Watchers brand and during the late 1990s Weight Watchers were active participants in Food in a Minute. This recipe shows how easy it is to create tasty, low-fat desserts.

8–10 medium-sized tamarillos
425 gram can Wattie's Boysenberries in Syrup
¼ cup flour
2 tblsp brown sugar
2 cups Weight Watchers Berry Flakes
2 tblsp butter, softened

1. Blanch, peel and slice the tamarillos.
2. Drain the boysenberries and reserve the juice.
3. Arrange the tamarillos and the boysenberries in a 6-cup capacity pie dish. Pour over about two-thirds of the juice. Heat the fruit either in a microwave for 3–5 minutes or oven for 15–20 minutes until hot. The fruit must be hot before the crumble goes on.
4. Sift the flour and brown sugar into a bowl. Stir through the berry flakes and rub in the butter. Do not worry if you are squashing the flakes, it's supposed to happen.
5. Sprinkle the crumble over the fruit. Bake at 190°C for 20–25 minutes until hot and golden.
6. Serve with yoghurt flavoured with a little of the remaining boysenberry juice.

Note: For individual serves, divide the mixture between 6 individual ramekins and bake for only 15 minutes.

Serves 6

Marmalade steamed pudding

Steamed puddings were even easier for families after this recipe aired as we cooked them in the microwave, taking only 5 minutes. Desserts don't get much easier than this.

50 grams butter
¼ cup sugar
1 egg
grated rind 1 lemon
1 cup self-raising flour, sifted
½ cup milk
6 tblsp Craig's Breakfast Marmalade
Meadow Fresh Sweetened Thickened Cream to accompany

1. Beat the butter and sugar together, then beat in the egg and lemon rind.

2. Stir in the flour and the milk.

3. Place 1½ tablespoons of marmalade in the base of 4 well-greased cups. Divide the batter among the cups.

4. Cook in the microwave on medium power for 5 minutes or until the puddings are cooked. (Or place the marmalade in the base of a well-greased steamed pudding basin and spoon the batter on top. Cover with 2 layers of baking or greaseproof paper and secure with string. Sit on a trivet or saucer in a large pot of boiling water and steam for 1 hour.)

5. Turn out onto a serving plate and serve with cream.

Serves 4

Index

A

Apples

Apple muesli 14
Apple muffins with spicy topping 174
Boysenberry apple crumble 200
No-fuss apple tart 178
Roast pork with sage and apple sauce 138
Sour cream apple pie 182
Sweet apple and pork braise 99

Asian beef kebabs 120
Asparagus slice 26
Autumn sausages 100
Autumn vegetables and bean korma curry 150

B

Bacon

Corn and bacon fritters on sweet chilli tomato 21
Creamy mushroom and bacon on pasta 44
Pumpkin and blue cheese fettuccine 49
Tomato and bean salad 162
Warm potato and bacon salad 165

Baked beans (and variants)

Autumn vegetable and bean korma curry 150
Baked bean hash 20
Baked bean lasagne 52
Beef and bean casserole 70
Boston baked beans 95
Chicken in pita with devilled baked beans 34
Chilli Mexicana 36
Father's day croissants 17
Mixed bean falafels with minted yoghurt 30
Moroccan-style beef and beans 75
Quick and easy nachos 38
Tomato and bean salad 162

Barbecued apricot-glazed ham with mustard fruits 131
Barbecued pork loin with sage and onion roasters 136
Barbecued sticky glazed spareribs 137

Beef

Asian beef kebabs 120
Beef and bean casserole 70
Chilli Mexicana 36
Country French meatballs 69
Flamenco pie 107
French beef and mushroom cottage pie 108
French country casserole 72
Glazed meatloaf 122
Herbed porcupines 73
Japanese-style stir-fried beef 61
Kumara and corned beef salad 163
Made-in-one-pan dinner 74
Mexican tortillas 37
Moroccan-style beef and beans 75
Quick and easy nachos 38
Tasty all-in-one meatballs 76
Tasty beef bolognese 77
Tex Mex tacos 39
Thai-scented burgers 124
Weekday curry 142
Winter beef casserole 78

Berry nice smoothie 22
Black doris plum self-saucing pudding 196
Blackberry bread and butter pudding 197
Blueberry chocolate cake 168
Blueberry jam muffins 176
Boston baked beans 95
Boysenberry apple crumble 200
Boysenberry ripple cake with custard 169
Breakfast pizzas 16
Butter chicken 143

C

Caesar-style salad 156

Cakes

Blueberry chocolate cake 168
Boysenberry ripple cake with custard 169
Carrot and orange cake 170
Chocolate berry cheesecake 189
Three berry chocoholics cake 172
Vanilla and boysenberry ice-cream cake 191
Yoghurt and pear syrup cake 173

Carrot and orange cake 170
Cheat's lasagne 53
Cheat's soufflé 27

Cheese

Cheesy corn frittata 32
Easy macaroni cheese 48
Macaroni cheese bake 97
Pumpkin and blue cheese fettuccine 49
Salami and feta gnocchi 50
Spinach and feta filo pie 106
Tomato, smoked tuna and feta pizza 56
Winter frittata 33

Chicken

Butter chicken 143
Chicken and spinach pies 109
Chicken in a pot 80
Chicken in pita with devilled baked beans 34
Chicken with mustard crème fraîche sauce 81

- Coconut chicken 125
- Cranberry and chicken pie 110
- Creamy chicken and corn pie 112
- Creamy smoked chicken filo pie 113
- Creamy sundried tomato stuffed chicken breasts 82
- Cumin and lemon baked chicken 84
- Devilled baked beans, with chicken in pita
- Easy chicken vegetable bake 83
- Herb roast chicken with sage and onion roasters 126
- Honey mustard and smoked chicken pasta salad 158
- Italian chicken and basil pasta 42
- Lemon chicken and spinach risotto 57
- Malay chicken satay on oriental rice 86
- Pumpkin and chicken pie 114
- Smoked chicken and melon salad 160
- Smoked chicken and tango chutney pizza 55
- Sweet and sour chicken 87
- Sweet chilli chicken with pawpaw salsa 127
- Tuscan chicken 88
- Warm chicken, grape and herb salad 160
- Winter chicken pie 115

Chickpea and pumpkin casserole 68
Chilli Mexicana 36
Chocolate
- Blueberry chocolate cake 168
- Chocolate berry cheesecake 189
- No-cook chocolate Christmas pudding 186
- Three berry chocoholics cake 172

Chuckwagon hash fritters 18
Coconut chicken 125
Corn
- Cheat's soufflé 27
- Cheesy corn frittata 32
- Chuckwagon hash fritters 18
- Corn and bacon fritters on sweet chilli tomato 21
- Creamy chicken and corn pie 112
- Mexican tortillas 37

Country French meatballs 69
Country lamb casserole 89
Cranberry and chicken pie 110
Cranberry turkey 128
Creamy boysenberry pudding 185
Creamy chicken and corn pie 112
Creamy mushroom and bacon on pasta 44
Creamy mushroom risotto 58
Creamy pumpkin pasta 46
Creamy smoked chicken filo pie 113
Creamy strawberry and amaretti dessert 185
Creamy sundried tomato stuffed chicken breasts 82
Creamy tropical muffins 177
Crunchy fish nuggets with dips 28
Cumin and lemon baked chicken 84
Curried lamb pies with ginger kumara mash 145
Curried winter vegetables 152

E
Easy chicken vegetable bake 83
Easy macaroni cheese 48

F
Father's day croissants 17
Fish
- Crunchy fish nuggets with dips 28
- Fish in sweet curry sauce 144
- Lemon-scented dory with tomato and garlic pasta 45
- Salmon hash cakes 24
- Smoked fish pie with garlic bread crust 116
- Spinach, lemon and tuna pilaf 60
- Thai-style calamari with Asian greens 62
- Tomato and vegetable pizza with tuna topping 56
- Tomato, smoked tuna and feta pizza 56

Flamenco pie 107
French beef and mushroom cottage pie 108
French country casserole 72
French salad 157
Fruit
- Apple muesli 14
- Apple muffins with spicy topping 174
- Barbecued apricot-glazed ham with mustard fruits 131
- Berry nice smoothie 24
- Boysenberry ripple cake with custard 169
- Chocolate berry cheesecake 189
- Creamy boysenberry pudding 185
- Creamy strawberry and amaretti dessert 185
- Creamy tropical muffins 177
- Grilled bananas with apricot sauce 194
- Minted tropical fruit salad 193
- No-fuss apple tart 178
- One crust fruit pie 180
- Orange and mango cheesecake ice-cream 190
- Quick trifle 192
- Roast pork with sage and apple sauce 138
- Smoked chicken and melon salad 160
- Sour cream apple pie 182
- Summer peach and cream cheese slice 184
- Sweet apple and pork braise 99
- Tamarillo and boysenberry crumble 201
- Tropical smoothie 24
- Vanilla and boysenberry ice-cream cake 191
- Yoghurt and pear syrup cake 173

Fruity blueberry self-saucing pudding 198
Fruity devilled sausages 101

G
Glazed meatloaf 122
Gnocchi, salami and feta 50
Golden plum pork loin chops 96
Greek-style salad 157
Grilled bananas with apricot sauce 194

H
Ham
Barbecued apricot-glazed ham with mustard fruits 131
Easy macaroni cheese 48
Ham with orange, sweet chilli and rum glaze
Macaroni cheese bake 97
New Zealand ham with orange, sweet chilli and rum glaze 132
Hearty lamb shanks 90
Herb roast chicken with sage and onion roasters 126
Herbed porcupines 73
Honey mustard and smoked chicken pasta salad 158

I
Indian pork korma 147
Italian chicken and basil pasta 42

J
Japanese-style stir-fried beef 61

K
Kumara
Curried lamb pies with ginger kumara mash 145
Kumara and corned beef salad 163
Tropical baked kumara 164

L
Lamb
Country lamb casserole 89
Curried lamb pies with ginger kumara mash 145
Hearty lamb shanks 90
Lamb curry with potatoes and spinach 146
Lamb provençale 91
Lea & Perrins ginger lamb chops 133
Moroccan lamb 92
Moroccan lamb pilaf 93
Quick winter roast lamb 134
Tuscan lamb shanks 94
Lea & Perrins ginger lamb chops 133
Lemon chicken and spinach risotto 57
Lemon-scented dory with tomato and garlic pasta 45
Lentil and vegetable butter curry 151
Lunchbox roll-ups 25

M
Macaroni cheese bake 97
Made-in-one-pan dinner 74
Malay chicken satay on oriental rice 86
Marmalade steamed pudding 202
Mexican tortillas 37
Mince
Chilli Mexicana 36
Country French meatballs 69
Flamenco pie 107
French beef and mushroom cottage pie 108
Glazed meatloaf 122
Herbed porcupines 73
Made-in-one-pan dinner 74
Moroccan-style beef and beans 75
Tasty all-in-one meatballs 76
Tex Mex tacos 39
Thai-scented burgers 124
Weekday curry 142
Minted tropical fruit salad 193
Mixed bean falafels with minted yoghurt 30
Moroccan lamb 92
Moroccan lamb pilaf 93
Moroccan-style beef and beans 75
Muesli, apple 14
Muffins
Apple muffins with spicy topping 174
Blueberry jam muffins 176
Creamy tropical muffins 177

N
New Zealand ham with orange, sweet chilli and rum glaze 132
No-cook chocolate Christmas pudding 186
No-fuss apple tart 178
Nutty banoffee pie 179

O
One crust fruit pie 180
Orange and mango cheesecake ice-cream 190
Oriental plum pizza with hummus 54

P
Pasta
Baked bean lasagne 52
Cheat's lasagne 53
Creamy mushroom and bacon on pasta 44
Creamy pumpkin pasta 46
Easy macaroni cheese 48
Honey mustard and smoked chicken pasta salad 158
Italian chicken and basil pasta 42
Lemon-scented dory with tomato and garlic pasta 45
Macaroni cheese bake 97
Pumpkin and blue cheese fettuccine 49
Peanut slice 183
Pizza pie 29
Pork
Barbecued pork loin with sage and onion roasters 136
Barbecued sticky glazed spareribs 137
Boston baked beans 95
Golden plum pork loin chops 96
Indian pork korma 147
Roast Pork with sage and apple sauce 138
Spanish pork chops with Mediterranean vegetable roasters 98

Sweet and sour oriental pork 63
Sweet apple and pork braise 99
Thai green pork curry 148

Potatoes
Lamb curry with potatoes and spinach 146
Warm potato and bacon salad 165

Pumpkin
Baked bean lasagne 52
Chickpea and pumpkin casserole 68
Creamy pumpkin pasta 46
Pumpkin and blue cheese fettuccine 49
Pumpkin and chicken pie 114

Q
Queen rice pudding 188
Quick and easy nachos 38
Quick trifle 192
Quick winter roast lamb 134

R
Rice
Creamy mushroom risotto 58
Lemon chicken and spinach risotto 57
Malay chicken satay on oriental rice 86
Moroccan lamb pilaf 93
Queen rice pudding 188
Spinach, lemon and tuna pilaf 60
Roast pork with sage and apple sauce 138
Roast turkey with oriental plum stuffing 129
Russian salad 159

S
Salami and feta gnocchi 50
Salmon hash cakes 24
Sausages
Autumn sausages 100
Fruity devilled sausages 101
Russian salad 159
Sausage hot pot 102
Winter sausages 104
Smoked chicken and melon salad 160
Smoked chicken and tango chutney pizza 55
Smoked fish pie with garlic bread crust 116
Sour cream apple pie 182
Spanish pork chops with Mediterranean vegetable roasters 98
Spinach
Cheat's lasagne 53
Chicken and spinach pies 109
Lamb curry with potatoes and spinach 146
Lemon chicken and spinach risotto 57
Spinach and feta filo pie 106
Spinach, lemon and tuna pilaf 60
Winter frittata 33
Summer peach and cream cheese slice 184
Sweet and sour chicken 87
Sweet and sour oriental pork 63
Sweet apple and pork braise 99
Sweet chilli chicken with pawpaw salsa 127

T
Tamarillo and boysenberry crumble 201
Tasty all-in-one meatballs 76
Tasty beef bolognese 77
Tex Mex tacos 39
Thai green pork curry 148
Thai-scented burgers 124
Thai-scented roast Christmas turkey 130
Thai-style calamari with Asian greens 62
Three berry chocoholics cake 172
Tomato and bean salad 162
Tomato and vegetable pizza with tuna topping 56
Tomato, smoked tuna and feta pizza 56
Tropical baked kumara 164
Tropical smoothie 22
Turkey
Cranberry turkey 128
Roast turkey with oriental plum stuffing 129
Thai-scented roast Christmas turkey 130
Tuscan chicken 88
Tuscan lamb shanks 94

V
Vanilla and boysenberry ice-cream cake 191
Vegetarian
Autumn vegetable and bean korma curry 150
Chickpea and pumpkin casserole 68
Chuckwagon hash fritters 18
Creamy mushroom risotto 58
Creamy pumpkin pasta 46
Curried winter vegetables 152
French salad 157
Greek-style salad 157
Lentil and vegetable butter curry 151
Mixed bean falafels with minted yoghurt 30
Spinach and feta filo pie 106

W
Warm chicken, grape and herb salad 160
Warm potato and bacon salad 165
Weekday curry 142
Winter beef casserole 78
Winter chicken pie 115
Winter frittata 33
Winter sausages 104

Y
Yoghurt and pear syrup cake 173